T0283061

THE ART AND SCIENCE OF
SUSHI

A COMPREHENSIVE GUIDE TO INGREDIENTS, TECHNIQUES AND EQUIPMENT

Technical Director **Jun Takahashi**
Supervisor **Hidemi Sato**
Text **Mitose Tsuchida**

TUTTLE Publishing
Tokyo | Rutland, Vermont | Singapore

Contents

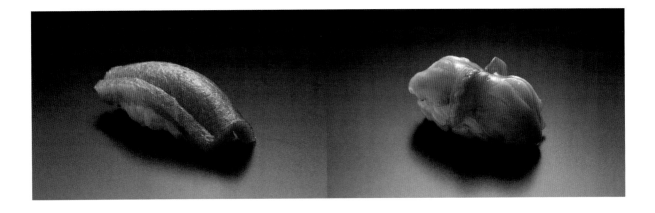

A Brief History of Sushi

The term *sushi* is now used worldwide for what is originally known by the Japanese as *nigirizushi* (an oblong mound of rice with a topping), a style of sushi that was only popularized in Japan in the twentieth century. Although nigirizushi has existed in Japan since the late eighteenth century, that was only in the city of Edo, now known as Tokyo. Types of sushi or sushi-like foods that were not balls of rice topped with fish existed around the country. If we explore the history of sushi in Japan, whether nigirizushi or other types of sushi, we get back to a food called *narezushi*, where fish and rice are fermented together.

The origins of sushi

Although sushi is known throughout the world these days, many people think sushi originated as sashimi raw fish fillets placed on top of rice. If you define sushi as "using raw fish" and "a topping for rice" it's inevitable that you would think that was the origin of sushi, but there are vegetable-only sushi types such as *inarizushi* (sushi rice stuffed into simmered fried tofu pockets), and there are types of fermented sushi where the fish is pressed onto the rice rather than placed on a rice ball, such as *funazushi* from Shiga Prefecture and *kaburazushi* from the Hokuriku region in northeastern Japan. Also, if you think of sushi as "a food that uses vinegar" or "a food that has a sour flavor because of fermentation," then this is true. The literal definition of sushi is "a food that is sour." One theory is that the original Japanese word for sushi is 酸し, meaning "sour."

Let's talk about the etymology of the word sushi. In kanji characters, it is and has been written as 寿し, 鮨, 寿司, 鮓, 寿之, 寿志 and 寿斗 to give a few examples. The most commonly used characters nowadays are 鮨, 鮓 or 寿司 (all read as *sushi*). Of the first two, 鮨 is in common use in the Kanto region around Tokyo, and 鮓 is used in the Kansai region around Osaka and Kyoto. The term 寿司 is an example of *ateji*, where random kanji characters are assigned to a word because of the way they are read rather than their meaning.

The term 鮨 has a very long history. In the Chinese dictionary called the *Erya* that dates back to the third century BCE, you can find the following definition: "Items made from fish are called 鮨 (*ki*), and items made from meat are called 醢 (*kai*)." In this context this term was applied to chopped and fermented fish, which is called *shiokara* in modern Japanese. If sushi could be confused with shiokara, it must have been quite liquid and gooey.

On the other hand, the term 鮓 is defined in another Chinese dictionary, the *Shuowen Jiezi* which dates back to the second century, as "A food where fish is pickled in rice and salt and weighted down with a stone." The tome also declares that this was valued as a fermented, long-keeping preserved food.

The terms 鮨 and 鮓 as used in the ancient dictionaries above referred to different foods. But in the third-century Chinese dictionary the *Guangya*, the two terms are mixed up, and as time passed they continued to be confused with each other in both China and Japan. Both 鮨 and 鮓 came to mean "A food where fish is pickled in rice and salt and weighted down with a stone." This is what is now called *narezushi*—a preserved food where lactic acid is created by naturally fermenting a starch such as rice, and where sourness inhibits the growth of rot-causing bacteria.

Narezushi and funazushi

Various types of *narezushi* (fish and rice fermented together) were passed down in several regions of Japan. The time periods during which such sushi became known differs by region, but quintessential narezushi types still made today include *funazushi*, made around Lake Biwa in Shiga Prefecture, *ayuzushi* from Gifu Prefecture, and *hishiko* from Fukui Prefecture. The words 鮒鮓, meaning *funazushi*, were found on a wooden record-keeping plaque that was discovered in the remains of Heijo-kyo, the old capital of Japan during the Nara period (710–794), so it's thought that it had been made even before then. The way it was made probably differs from the way it's made now, but it was still a narezushi, made by putting fish or seafood together with rice and allowing it to ferment.

Funazushi is traditionally made in Shiga Prefecture with *nigoro buna* carp, spawning in Lake Biwa between February and May. First the fish is preserved in salt. Around late July, the fish is desalted and put up with rice for the main pickling process. First rice is spread out on the bottom of a barrel and then spread with a layer of carp that have been stuffed with more rice. Another layer of rice is spread on top of that, and then another layer of stuffed carp. This is repeated several times, then the layers are covered and weighted down with stones to mature.

The word 鮓 is circled in red on the left-hand record-keeping plaque at Takahama Town Hall, Fukui Prefecture, which notes that sushi made with mussels in a pot-like vessel called a *kaku* was received as a tribute from the Kizu region, (present-day Kinki region, around Osaka and Kyoto). Photo credit: Takahama Town Hall.

Not only does the lactic acid produced inhibit the growth of harmful bacteria, fermenting the fish produces an abundance of umami, which imparts a unique flavor. Only the fish is eaten, and the rice is discarded.

Funazushi is usually fermented for three to six months, sometimes for as long as two years. With this long fermentation time the rice turns into an inedible liquid goo. So at some point the during the Muromachi period (1336–1573) and Azuchi Momoyama period (1568–1600), "raw narezushi"—where the fermentation time was shortened and the fish and rice were eaten together—was born. (The *ayuzushi* from Gifu Prefecture is of this type.) Later, in order to hasten fermentation, rice *koji* (rice inoculated with the *Aspergillus oryzae* mold) was mixed into the rice, and vegetables were added in with the fish too. This type of sushi is called *izushi*, and the kaburazushi mentioned on page 6 is of this type.

Eventually, vinegar made its appearance in sushi. Vinegar has been around in Japan since ancient times, but it was discovered that by adding it to rice, one could enjoy a sour flavor without waiting for it to ferment. While sushi started out as something that needed time to ferment naturally in the form of narezushi and izushi, the rice came to be eaten along with the fish, vinegar was introduced, and quickly-made vinegared rice or sushi rice was born. This led to a big change in the way sushi was made.

The birth of bakozushi and nigirizushi

By the Edo period (1603–1868) sushi was no longer a preserved food. *Hayazushi* or "one-night sushi" was introduced. First off, *sugatazushi* and *kokerazushi* (which are related to the *hakozushi* pressed sushi prevalent in the Kansai region) were born, followed by *makizushi* or sushi rolls, *inarizushi* or sushi rice stuffed into fried tofu skins, and *chirashizushi*, where various ingredients are placed on top of or mixed into the rice.

Kokerazushi is made by packing vinegared sushi rice into a box, topping it with filleted fish and pressing it down. This then began to be cut up into easy-to-eat pieces. Each of these small pieces was then wrapped in bamboo leaves and weighted down—this is *kenukizushi*, which is thought to be the predecessor of the present-day *sasamakizushi*, sushi wrapped in bamboo leaves. Sasamakizushi is thought to be the ancestor of Edomae *nigirizushi* (a topping on a ball of sushi rice). The term

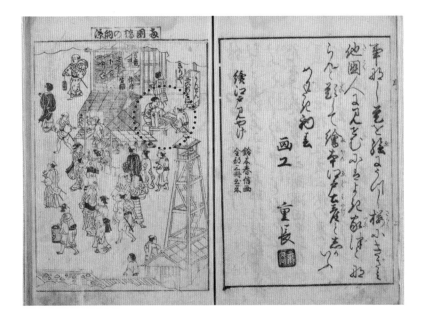

A sushi seller's stall (circled in red) is depicted in this illustration entitled "Enjoying the Cool Evening Air at Ryogoku Bridge" from the eighteenth-century *Edo Gifts Picture Book*. (Photo credit: National Diet Library)

A painting of sushi by nihonga artist Kawabata Gyokusho from the Meiji period (1868–1912). The red fish in the center that looks like tuna is actually sea trout. (From the collection of Yoshinozushi; excerpted from *Sushi Technique Textbook*, Edomae Sushi chapter, Asahiya Publishing)

"Edomae" refers to the style of sushi that became popular in Tokyo in the Edo period.

There are various theories as to when nigirizushi was introduced, but the most common one is that a sushi seller in the Ryogoku district of Edo (the old name for Tokyo) called Hanaya Yohei was the first to offer nigirizushi at his establishment, Yohei Zushi. This was in the latter part of the Edo period, when ships from other countries were heading to Japan and demanding that the country opened up to foreign trade. At this time, the country had a thriving urban culture with Edo as its center: theater, *ukiyo-e* woodblock prints, literature and other sources of entertainment were in full bloom. Edo had become a huge city to which many people came seeking work, and establishments serving food became fashionable. Amongst those were sushi stalls. Nigirizushi, which could be made quickly, was a "fast food" that became popular amongst the people of Edo. The nigirizushi of the period were not the small bite-sized portions we know today, but were as large as *onigiri* rice balls are now. The most popular type of fish used was *kohada* or gizzard shad, and "kohada sellers" who walked around with barrels of this fish for sale helped to make the streets of Edo lively.

As nigirizushi gained popularity in Edo, *hakozushi* (pressed sushi) became less popular there, and by the Meiji period (1868–1912) and Taisho period (1912–1926) it was commonly said "Kansai is hakozushi, Kanto is nigirizushi."

From food stalls to indoor restaurants

As a carryover from the end of the Edo period, street food stalls known as *yatai* continued to be popular in the Meiji period. Eventually some establishments that served sushi indoors appeared, called *uchimise*, characterized by the fact that customers stood while chefs made the sushi kneeling down in the formal *seiza* position. This is because at the beginning of the twentieth century, most uchimise sushi establishments were delivery and takeout places.

Whether the place was a food stall or an indoor establishment, refrigeration did not exist yet, so care had to be taken that the fish would not go bad. In order for the customers to bring home their sushi safely from uchimise, or to keep the fish from spoiling at outdoor sushi stalls, the seafood and fish were salted, or marinated in vinegar or soy sauce, or cooked. And since the raw seafood and fish came from Edo (Tokyo) Bay, the work done to this seafood and fish was called "Edomae (*in front of Edo*) work."

Eventually ice became easier to obtain, and raw, unprocessed fish and seafood could be served on top of sushi rice. As these raw sushi types became more popular, uchimise started to offer them too, as well as providing seats for their clients so they could dine in. This was the beginning of the "sushi restaurant" as we know it today.

Sushi stalls still existed in the early years of the Showa period (1926–1989), but after the end of World War II, such food stalls disappeared due to concerns about food safety. There still exist some sushi restaurants where they hang *noren* curtains over their counters, instead of at the entrance door as is more usual; this is a legacy of the sushi stalls who hung their noren right over their counters.

After World War II, the environment around sushi changed drastically. With the spread of refrigeration, including industrial refrigerators, cooked or preserved sushi toppings became fewer, and raw fish toppings became the default. As freezing technology advanced, along with international trading routes, and fish and seafood started entering Japan from all around the world, the variety of sushi toppings increased. At an old-time sushi stall, only a few items of sushi were available, but these days there are more than twenty commonly seen toppings.

The amount of rice used has also changed. In order for the customer to eat a variety of raw fish, sushi balls have become smaller, and the style of eating sushi has changed so that one typically eats ten to twenty pieces of sushi at a sitting. And the flavor of the rice has become lighter in order to fully convey the subtle flavors of raw fish. Besides nigirizushi, a typical sushi restaurant nowadays serves a variety of appetizers and alcoholic drinks. And the *omakase* style of ordering, where one leaves the selection of sushi the diner eats to the chef, has also become popular along with *okonomi*, where the diner picks what they want. These days sushi is often enjoyed with wine, besides the usual beer and sake. Ever since a sushi restaurant made an appearance in the 2008 edition of the *Michelin Guide*, sushi restaurants have garnered worldwide attention, and the *Michelin Guide* lists more and more sushi establishments with every issue. The 2020 edition lists three 3-star sushi restaurants, seven 2-star ones, twenty-four 1-star places and four Bib Gourmand establishments.

The number of sushi restaurants has increased worldwide too, from "conveyor-belt"

東都名高廿六夜待與之杻圖

This woodblock print from the late Edo period "Famous Places of the Eastern Capital" by the great ukiyo-e artist Utagawa Hiroshige, shows people enjoying themselves in the Takanawa district of Edo, as they try to catch a glimpse of the moon rising over the sea. A variety of foods are offered by the food stalls such as dumplings, soba noodles and tempura. On the far right is a sushi stall. (Collection of the Tokyo Metropolitan Edo-Tokyo Museum. Image from the archives of the Tokyo Metropolitan Foundation for History and Culture)

establishments to high-end sushi restaurants. Expensive sushi restaurants located in big cities around the world appeal especially to the discerning customer and grab plenty of local attention.

It's been a long time since sushi made its appearance in this world, but thanks to the expertise of many, it has evolved into a food that typifies Japanese cuisine today. The sushi that has traveled over the sea to other lands has the potential to continue to become deeply rooted in those countries, as it melds with the culture there.

Sushi Toppings

The color of the fish changes with the seasons, as it waits quietly on the cutting board, in the glass display case, or in the toppings box.

鯛
TAI / Sea Bream

鮃
HIRAME / Olive Flounder

春子
KASUGO / Young Sea Bream

鰈
KAREI / Right-Eye Flounder

鮪／中トロ
CHUTORO / Medium Marbled Tuna Belly

鮪／大トロ
OTORO / Premium Marbled Tuna Belly

鮪／赤身
AKAMI / Lean Tuna

漬け
ZUKE / Marinated Tuna

鰹
KATSUO / Skipjack Tuna

鰯
IWASHI / Sardine

縞鯵
SHIMA-AJI / Striped Jack

鯵
AJI / Horse Mackerel

小肌
KOHADA / Gizzard Shad

鯖
SABA / Mackerel

細魚
SAYORI / Halfbeak

海松貝
MIRUGAI / Gaper Clam

赤貝
AKAGAI / Ark Clam

鮑
AWABI / Abalone

小柱
KOBASHIRA / Surf Clam Scallop

鳥貝
TORIGAI / Egg Cockle

蛤
HAMAGURI / Asian Hard Clam

墨烏賊
SUMI-IKA / Golden Cuttlefish

障泥烏賊
AORI-IKA / Bigfin Reef Squid

蛸
TAKO / Octopus

甘海老
AMAEBI / Sweet Shrimp

牡丹海老
BOTAN EBI / Botan Shrimp

車海老
KURUMA EBI / Tiger Shrimp

蝦蛄
SHAKO / Mantis Shrimp

いくら
IKURA / Salmon Roe

雲丹
UNI / Sea Urchin

穴子
ANAGO / Conger Eel

玉子焼き
TAMAGOYAKI / Japanese Omelet

Seasonality of Seafood in Japan

Although delicious sushi toppings can be eaten all year round thanks to modern preservation methods and global trading, the fish and seafood that can be caught in season around the shores of Japan's long coastline, is really exceptional.

Sushi Topping	Month	January	February	March	April
White Fish	Sea Bream				
	Olive Flounder				
	Young Sea Bream				
	Right-Eye Flounder				
Red Fish	Tuna	5th: first auction		From Australia	
	Skipjack Tuna				First catch
Blue-skinned Fish	Sardine				
	Striped Jack				
	Horse Mackerel				
	Gizzard Shad				
	Mackerel				
	Halfbeak				
Shellfish	Gaper				
	Ark Clam				
	Abalone				
	Surf Clam Scallop				
	Egg Cockle				
	Asian Hard Clam				
Squid, Octopus, Shrimp	Golden Cuttlefish				
	Bigfin Reef Squid				
	Octopus				
	Sweet Shrimp				
	Botan Shrimp				
	Tiger shrimp				
	Mantis Shrimp				
Fish Eggs, Conger Eel	Salmon Roe				
	Sea Urchin				
	Conger Eel				

May	June	July	August	September	October	November	December
From New Zealand		From Boston, USA		Domestic			
				Returning catch			
		Small shad					
		First catch					

Fisheries Map

Thanks to its long coastline, good quality fish has been caught around Japan since ancient times. The birth of sushi that uses fresh, raw fish was a very natural development. There are certain areas that are well-known for certain species of fish. This page shows Japan's main fisheries and the fish they are known for.

Migratory Movement of Tuna

- Summer to fall (moving north)
- Fall to winter (moving south)
- Main fisheries for bluefin tuna

Rebun
Rishiri
Mashike
Tokoro
Yoichi
Otaru
Hiroo
Tomakomai
Okushiri
Setana
Urakawa
Shiriuchi
Toi
Oma
Tappizaki
Minmaya
Hachinohe
Ofunato
Shichigahama
Kesennuma
Shiogama
Ishinomaki
Sado Island
Yuriage
Niigata
Somaharagama
Toyama
Kashima
Sakaiminato
Maisaka
Kuwana
Hinase
Akashi
Yaizu
Imabari
Awaji
Mikawa Bay
Omaezaki
Tsushima
Kannonji
Kada
Iki
Hiji
Naruto
Tara
Ariake
Susami
Kushimoto
Nachikatsuura
Goto Islands
Oita
Nagasaki
Saganoseki
Ainan
Amakusa
Izumi
Kawaminami
Aburatsu
Miyazaki

Izu/Ogasawara route

Kishuu offshore route

Kuroshio
Current route

**Northern Migration
Routes of Tuna**

Rausu
Nemuro
Akkeshi

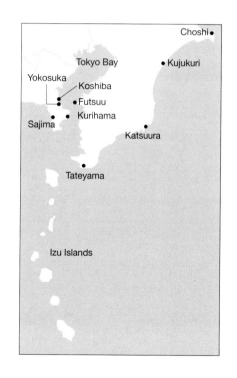

Choshi
Tokyo Bay
Kujukuri
Yokosuka
Koshiba
Futsuu
Sajima
Kurihama
Katsuura
Tateyama
Izu Islands

* Includes fish farms. Differs depending on the time of the year.
* Although fish are imported from around the world, this chart lists the main domestic fisheries that supply sushi restaurants around Japan.

The main fisheries for the sushi toppings in this book	
Sea Bream	Wakayama (Kada), Seto Inland Sea (Naruto, Awaji, Imabari)
Olive Flounder	Hokkaido (Setana), Chiba (Choshi), Aomori (Hachinohe)
Young Sea Bream	Tokyo Bay, Hyogo (Awaji), Kagoshima (Izumi)
Right-Eye Flounder	Tokyo Bay, Hyogo (Awaji), Kagoshima (Izumi)
Skipjack Tuna	Miyagi (Ishinomaki), Chiba (Katsuura), Wakayama (Susami), Miyazaki (Aburatsu)
Sardine	Chiba (Choshi), Shizuoka (Yaizu), Wakayama (Kushimoto), Tottori (Sakaiminato)
Striped Jack	Chiba (Sotobo), Tokyo (Izu Islands), Wakayama (Kushimoto), Ehime (Ainan)
Horse Mackerel	Chiba (Futtsu), Oita (Saganoseki), Kagochima (Izumi)
Gizzard Shad	Tokyo Bay, Shizuoka (Maisaka), Saga (Tara), Kumamoto (Amakusa)
Mackerel	Miyagi (Ishinomaki), Chiba (Futtsu), Tottori (Sakaiminato), Oita (Saganoseki)
Halfbeak	Miyagi (Shichigahama), Aichi (Mikawa Bay), Hyogo (Awaji)
Gaper Clam	Tokyo Bay, Aichi (Mikawa Bay)
Ark Clam	Miyagi (Yuriage), Kagawa (Kannonji), Oita
Abalone	Chiba (Uchibo, Sotobo)
Surf Clam Scallop	Hokkaido (Tomakomai, Okushiri)
Egg Cockle	Aichi (Mikawa Bay), Tokyo Bay, Kagawa (Kannonji)
Asian Hard Clam	Ibaraki (Kashima), Chiba (Kujukuri), Aichi (Kuwana)
Golden Cuttlefish	Kumamoto (Amakusa), Kagoshima (Izumi)
Bigfin Reef Squid	Nagasaki (Goto Islands), Chiba (Tateyama), Shizuoka (Omaezaki)
Octopus	Kanagawa (Sajima, Kurihama), Hyogo (Akashi), Nagasaki
Sweet Shrimp	Hokkaido (Yoichi), Niigata, Toyama
Botan Shrimp	Hokkaido (Mashike), Toyama
Tiger Shrimp	Tokyo Bay, Oita, Kumamoto (Amakusa), Miyazaki
Mantis Shrimp	Hokkaido (Otaru), Tokyo Bay (Koshiba), Fukushima (Somaharagama), Okayama (Hinase)
Salmon Roe	Hokkaido (Tokoro, Rausu, Hiroo, Urakawa)
Sea Urchin	Hokkaido
Conger Eel	Miyagi (Ishinomaki), Tokyo Bay, Nagasaki (Tsushima)
Nori Seaweed	Nagasaki (Ariake)

The Sushi Counter

Making the sushi and eating the sushi. The counter of a sushi restaurant is where both of these activities take place. The chefs stand behind the counter, an area called the *tsukeba* in Japanese, and carry out their work, and the customers enjoy their every movement as if they are watching a stage performance. This kind of space is quite unique to a sushi restaurant.

CHAPTER 1

THE SCIENCE OF SUSHI (PART 1):
SEAFOOD AND HOW TO PREPARE IT

The Japanese Kitchen Knife

A key task at a sushi restaurant is preparing the fish and seafood that is brought in. In the kitchen the fish are filleted and cut into blocks, and at the counter the blocks of fish are sliced in front of the customers. Once a cut is made into the fish it can not be undone; this is job that requires the utmost concentration.

Japanese Kitchen Knife (*Hocho*)

The knife is indispensable for preparing and slicing fish, and is an extension of the chef's hands. A glossy, smooth cut surface not only looks good, the "cut" of a knife really influences the taste and texture of the fish. Kitchen knives all have very different uses, and in Japan alone there are several dozen varieties. The knives in use in Japan can be divided into three general types: traditional *wa* or Japanese-style knives made using forging methods passed down through the generations; Western-style knives in wide use in home kitchens; and Chinese-style knives used at Chinese restaurants. Sushi restaurants usually use Japanese-style knives. The big difference between Japanese- and Western-style knives is the blade. Japanese-style knives usually have a *kataba* "one-sided blade," combining a soft iron with a hard iron called *hagane*. As the name indicates, the blade of the knife is on one side only. This side of the knife is very hard, and fish sliced with the hard, sharp blade has a very beautiful cut surface. On the other hand, Western-style blades are manufactured by stamping a sheet of iron, and have a *ryoba*, or blade on both sides of the knife. Since this style of knife is relatively easy to handle, it is widely used in home kitchens. Of all the Japanese-style knives available, sushi restaurants most often use the *deba bocho* knife and the *yanagiba bocho* knife.

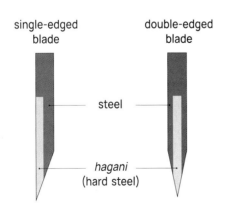

single-edged blade   double-edged blade

steel

hagani (hard steel)

The Blade Must Be Sharp

If a knife with a dull blade is used, the cut surface will not be clean, and both the taste and the texture of the fish will be affected. The photos below show the cut surfaces of tuna under a scanning electron microscope. When the tuna is cut with a sharp knife the surface is smooth, but when cut with a dull one it is rough.

Cut with a sharp sashimi knife   Cut with a sharp general purpose knife   Cut with a dull knife

Single-edged Knives

片刃包丁

Single-
Edged Knives
(*Kataba*)

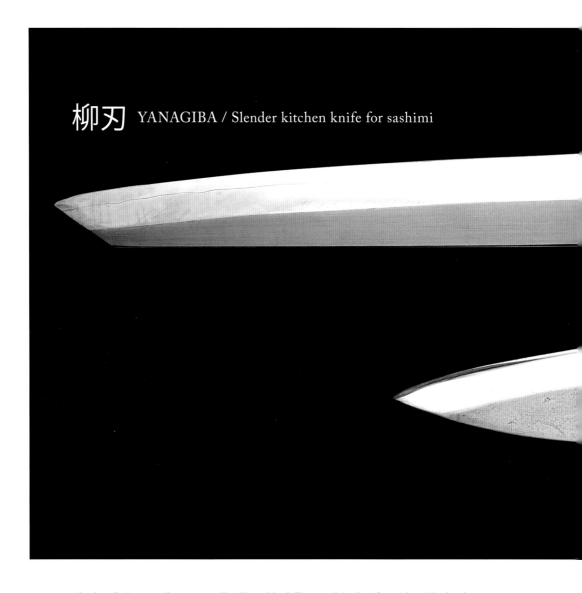

柳刃 YANAGIBA / Slender kitchen knife for sashimi

A *yanagiba* knife (*yanagiba* means "willow blade") is a thin knife with a blade that is about 9½ to 14 inches (24 to 36 cm) long, with a point. This very sharp blade produces beautiful cut surfaces, and is used to slice sashimi as well as sushi toppings. Because of its long blade, it can cut through in one motion without having to use a sawing movement, resulting in that smooth cut surface. It is stabilized by holding the index finger on the back of the blade, and gripping the handle with the other fingers. While using this knife it is important to take into account the grain of what is being cut. Steady your breath, and try to use the whole blade to make the cut in one smooth flow.

出刃 DEBA / Broad-bladed carving knife

A *deba* knife is a thick, broad knife (*deba* means "blade that sticks out"). It is generally used to break down fish. Since it has weight, it's ideal for cutting off the head of the fish or slicing through bones. Deba knives come in various sizes, ranging from small ones around 4 inches (10 cm) long to large ones around 9½ inches (24 cm) long, with the sizes going up in approximately 1 inch (3 cm) increments. To use the knife, place the index finger on the back of the blade, and the middle finger in the indentation under the heel of the blade, with the ring and little fingers wrapped around the handle.

The Parts of a Japanese Kitchen Knife

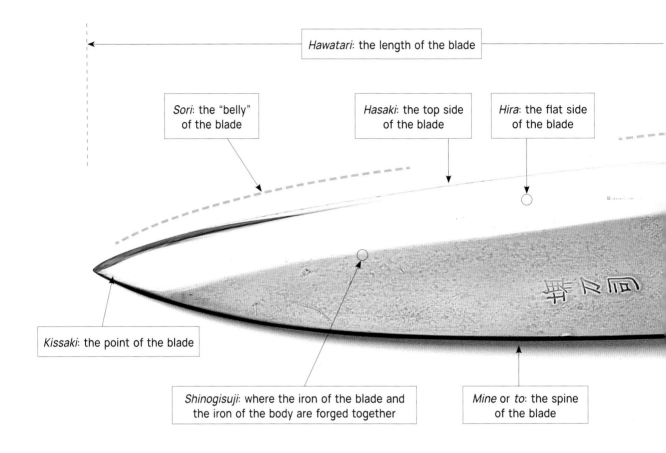

Hawatari: the length of the blade

Sori: the "belly" of the blade

Hasaki: the top side of the blade

Hira: the flat side of the blade

Kissaki: the point of the blade

Shinogisuji: where the iron of the blade and the iron of the body are forged together

Mine or *to*: the spine of the blade

Making a traditional Japanese knife: the steps

1. Forging and welding
This is the process of welding the *hagane* (hard steel) of the blade to the soft steel of the body of the knife. Sodium borate and iron oxide powder are sprinkled onto the soft steel as a adherent, a small piece of hagane is placed on it and the blade is heated to 1650°F (900°C) while being beaten with a hammer to shape it.

2. Rough finish
The bends and twists created during the welding process are corrected, and extra bits are cut or ground off in order to shape the blade.

3. Hardening
A powder made from ground sharpening stones is painted onto the blade and dried before the blade is heated to 1470°F (800°C), then cooled rapidly in water. This hardens the steel.

Why Is a Yanagiba Knife So Long?

Experiments have shown that a cut surface sliced with a long knife such as a yanagiba (page 24) is more beautiful than one cut with a short blade. Although it takes longer to cut using a yanagiba knife, its long blade causes less damage to the fibers of whatever is being cut, while smoothing out its surface, making it shiny.

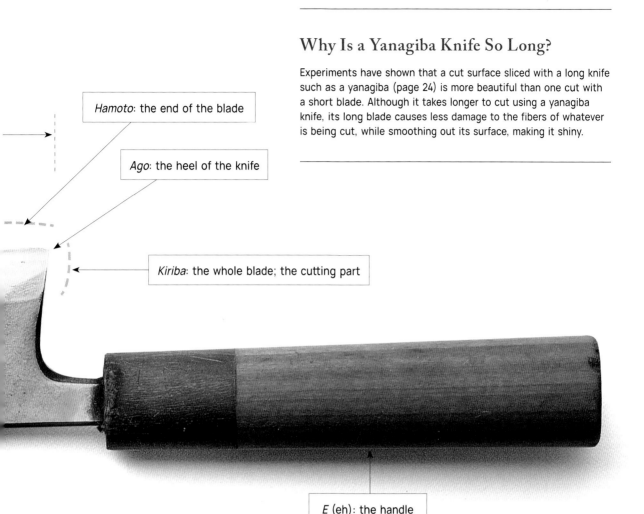

Hamoto: the end of the blade

Ago: the heel of the knife

Kiriba: the whole blade; the cutting part

E (eh): the handle

4. Tempering and breaking in the blade

Step 3 hardens the blade, but makes it very brittle. Next, it is tempered by heating it to 300–390°F (150–200°C), then cooled slowly to restore its strength and flexibility. The balance between hardness and flexibility is an important factor in determining the cut of the blade, and it's said that this is the most difficult step of all. After tempering the blade, any leftover dirt or powder is removed, and any irregularities are corrected by hammering. This latter step is called *narashi*, breaking in the blade.

5. Sharpening and attaching the handle

The blade is sharpened, first with a coarse grinding stone , then moving to finer and finer ones. Since the blade heats up during this grinding process, it is cooled with water to prevent it becoming warped or chipped. Finally the handle is hammered on, and the knife is cleaned.

白身

White Fish
(*Shiromi*)

White Fish

Fish with white flesh and little of the red blood-rich parts called *chiai* are called *shiromi* or white-fleshed fish. Although white fish is light in flavor, it has umami, and the translucent, beautiful flesh is eaten raw as well as salted or marinated in kombu seaweed. Eaten together with sushi rice, it has a unique texture and flavor.

The standard types of white fish served at sushi restaurants that specialize in Edomae (traditional Tokyo-style) sushi are sea bream (*tai*) and the flounders (*hirame* and *karei*), but in recent years the variety of white fish has increased. These days you'll find sea bass (*suzuki*), flathead (*kochi*), filefish (*kawahagi*), gurnard (*hobo*), red snapper or splendid alfonsino (*kinmedai*), blowfish (*fugu*), monkfish (*anko*) and pike conger (*hamo*) added to the selection of sushi toppings. Good white fish has firm, dense flesh with a translucent quality. Although it is light in flavor, it has umami and sweetness and a faint yet distinct aroma. The popular olive flounder (*hirame*) sushi topping is made with fish killed using the *ikejime* method (see below), then filleted, wrapped in a cloth and rested in the refrigerator until it reaches a desirable consistency.

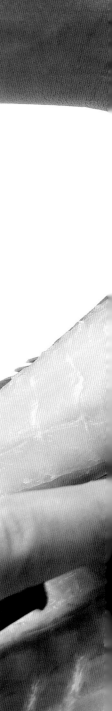

Killing the Fish for Maximum Flavor

If a fish struggles and flaps around a lot, the ATP that is the source of the inosinic acid where its umami comes from (see page 48-49) is used up. In order to prevent the reduction of ATP, the fish has to be prevented from struggling once it is caught. There are two methods for doing this, called *ikejime* and *shinkeijime*; basically both start with ikejime — instantly killing the fish — and if necessary, shinkeijime is also performed.

With the ikejime method, the spinal cord of the fish is either pierced with a handheld hook or severed with a knife. However when it comes to large fish, even if it quiets down after this, it may start moving around again after some time, reducing the ATP. In order to prevent this, a wire is inserted into the spinal cord to destroy the nervous system and to prevent any signals from being transmitted to the brain; this is called shinkeijime. By performing ikejime or shinkeijime, the ATP in the body of the fish is retained, which delays rigor mortis. After these procedures are performed, a knife is inserted behind the gills or into a vein near the tail of the fish to drain out the blood; this is called *chinuki*. Chinuki delays the discoloring of the flesh or the fishy odor that can arise after a fish is killed, resulting in delicious flesh that is clean, beautiful and packed with umami.

All About Sea Bream

The sea bream (*tai*) is a fish with soft flesh and very hard bones. Wild sea bream in particular has a part called the hemal spine, line of small bones that stretches from the back bone to the stomach. For this reason it's a fish that is hard to break down properly and easy to spoil with a knife, damaging the flesh. A *deba* knife (see page 25) is used to fillet the fish into three pieces: the back side, the front side and the bones. Since the part just under the skin is packed with umami and has a desirable crunchy texture, when sea bream is used for sushi, it is not only served with the skin removed, but is also served with the skin left on, after blanching the surface in boiling water.

Sea Bream (*Tai*)

What is red sea bream?

Although there are several types of fish in the sea bream category, in the sushi world a sea bream refers to what's called a *madai* or "true tai" (red sea bream, Pangrus major). It has a bright red color which looks great, and has been used on festive occasions in Japan for a long time. Although line-caught sea bream from the wild is highly prized for its quality, farmed sea bream is widely available too. Red sea bream has a lot of sweetness; it has more of the amino acid called glycine, which is the source of sweet flavor, than either skipjack tuna (*katsuo*) or tuna (*maguro*).

Amount of glycine per 3½ oz (100 grams)	
Red sea bream	8–34 mg
Skipjack tuna	4–7 mg
Tuna	3–8 mg

(Source: Japan Society of Nutrition and Food Science website, "Free amino acids in foods" chart)

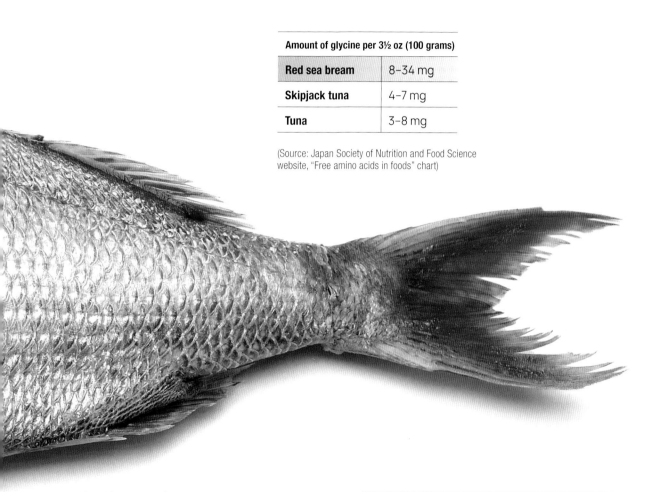

A scale remover is used to carefully remove all the scales from the fish. The tool is passed along the fish from the tail to the head in small strokes against the grain of the scales, to remove all of them except from the head and the belly. Change to a deba knife next (see page 25), and remove the scales from the belly side and around the head with care. The point of the knife is used to remove the scales from the top of the head and around the back fin.

Filleting a Fish into Three Pieces

Filleting a fish into three pieces — the back, the belly and the bones — is the most basic way of breaking it down. A *deba* knife (see page 25) is used for this task. Besides sea bream, this method is used for most other fish used as sushi toppings, including horse mackerel (*aji*) and skipjack tuna (*katsuo*), to divide the fish into the top or back side, bottom or belly side and the bones, with the back and belly parts being turned into *saku* or blocks that are then sliced for sashimi and sushi. Before the fish is filleted, the scales are removed, the innards are removed and washed out, and the head and tail are taken off. This pre-filleting procedure is called *mizu arai* or water-washing.

Water-washing steps

1 Remove the scales (see page 31).
2 Place the fish with the head facing right and the belly on the near side. Open up the gill flap and cut in, removing the head following the line there. Cut through the thin skin that attaches the gills to the head. Turn the fish over and repeat on the other side, cutting through the thin skin on that side too.
3 Open up the gill flap and insert the knife, cut off the base of the gills on the front and back and pull out the gills.
4 Remove the innards with the tip of the knife, from the

chin to the anus, taking care not to cut through them.
5 Pull the innards out with your hands, and sever them off with the knife.
6 Run the tip of the knife along the inner bone, and make a cut into the bloody part of the fish.
7 Rinse out the stomach of the fish under running water carefully. Pat dry with a kitchen cloth.
8 Make a cut along the line that connects the breast side fin to the back fin. Stop when the blade hits the bone. Turn the fish over, and repeat on the other side.
9 Put the knife on the bone where it connects the head to the body, and cut through it in one go to sever the head.

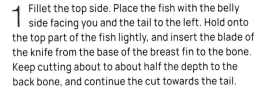

1 Fillet the top side. Place the fish with the belly side facing you and the tail to the left. Hold onto the top part of the fish lightly, and insert the blade of the knife from the base of the breast fin to the bone. Keep cutting about to about half the depth to the back bone, and continue the cut towards the tail.

2 When the cut reaches the tail, remove the blade and re-insert it from the head side. Lift up the top half of the fish lightly, and keep pulling it up in step with the movement and speed that you move the knife, as you keep cutting in towards the bone.

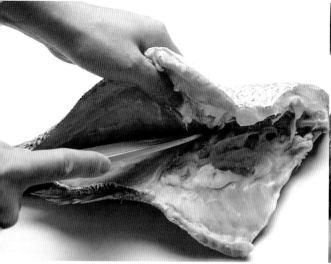

3 Keep advancing the knife little by little until it reaches the bone.

4 When the blade reaches the bone, flip around the fish so the tail is facing to the right and the back is towards you. Make a shallow cut on the back side towards the head.

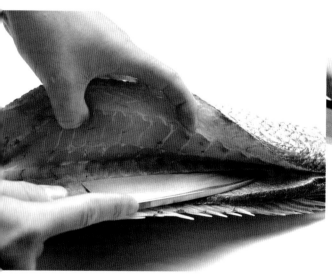

5 Lift the top half of the fish up lightly with one hand, and keep pulling it up in step with the movement and speed of your knife as you keep cutting in towards the bone to the head side. Continue moving the knife until the blade reaches the back bone.

6 Run the tip of the blade along the part of the back bone that rises up as you keep cutting.

7 Turn the blade around towards the tail, and cut through to the bone in one go. This removes the top fillet.

8 Flip the fish around again so the head side is facing right and the back facing towards you, and make a shallow cut towards the back bone.

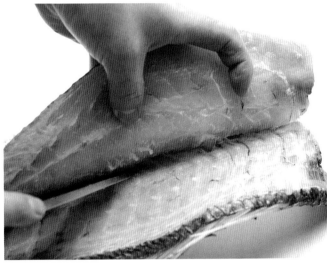

9 Lift the bottom half of the fish lightly with your hand, and keep pulling it up in step with the movement and speed of your knife as you keep cutting in towards the bone to the head side.

10 Continue moving the knife until the blade reaches the back bone.

11 Turn the fish around again so the tail is facing right with the belly side towards you. Cut through the belly side until the blade gets to the point where you cut through on the other side.

12 Turn the blade towards the tail end, and cut through in one go to remove the bottom fillet.

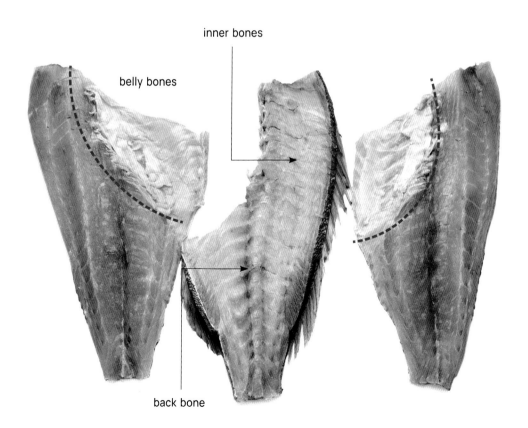

inner bones

belly bones

back bone

This is a three-part fillet: the top side, the inner bones, and the bottom side. The belly bones are then removed from the top and bottom fillets, and the skin is peeled off. The remaining parts are the *saku*, the parts that are used for sashimi and sushi.

All About Flounder

Flounders — the olive or left-eye flounder (*hirame*) and the right-eye flounder (*karei*) — are flat-bodied fish that live on the sea bed. Their flat bodies let them blend into the sea bed, making it difficult for predators to locate them. Although they look similar, as the names "left-eye flounder" and "right-eye flounder" indicate, you can tell them apart by the side on which their eyes are located. Since they have flat, wide bodies, they are cut into five pieces, with a cut made along the central bone first. Next the flesh is cut through on the belly and back sides in order not to damage it.

鮃

Olive Flounder (*Hirame*)

Wild olive flounders are in season from the late fall to early spring, getting fatter when the frosts descend on the land. Although they are also available from the spring to summer, many sushi restaurants won't use them because they are much leaner after they have spawned. The *engawa* or tail-fin muscle, of which only a small amount is available on each fish, has a crunchy texture because it is used a lot to move the back and belly fins, and is very popular as a sushi topping because of its umami and mouthfeel.

The scales on a flounder are very fine and cover the whole body densely. Therefore a yanagiba knife (see page 24) is used to shave them off thinly in a procedure called *sukibiki*. The scales on the black top skin as well as the white bottom skin are removed in this manner.

鰈

Right-Eye Flounder (*Karei*)

Although there are many types of right eyed flounders, the ones called marbled flounder (*makogarei*) and spotted halibut (*hoshigarei*) are the most popular as sushi toppings. The season for either of these caught in the wild is the summer, but of the two, spotted halibut is the rarest and is therefore very expensive. The appeal of this type of flounder is above all its texture. Because it is packed with collagen, it has a wonderful crunchy texture when it's eaten raw.

Filleting a Fish into Five Pieces

This method of filleting is used for flat fish, such as flounder. The fish is broken down into five pieces — two fillets each on both sides, and the bones. The *engawa* or the tail fin muscle is highly prized on its own as a sushi topping, so the fish is filleted carefully so as not to damage this part. The scales are removed before the fish is filleted with a yanagiba knife (see page 24), the innards are removed and rinsed out, and the head and tail are removed. This pre-filleting procedure is called *mizu arai*, or water-washing.

Water-Washing steps for flounder

1 Shave off the scales using a yanagiba knife. Any remaining scales are removed with a deba knife (see page 25).
2 Make a cut with a deba knife from the side of the breast fin along the line of the head. Turn the fish over and repeat on the other side. Remove the head from the fish along with the innards.
3 Rinse well, and pat dry.

1 Use a deba knife. Place the fish so the head side is facing diagonally up to the right. Hold the fish down lightly with your left hand and make a straight cut in the middle of the fish above the back bone.

2 Make a shallow cut along the edge of the fins around the body.

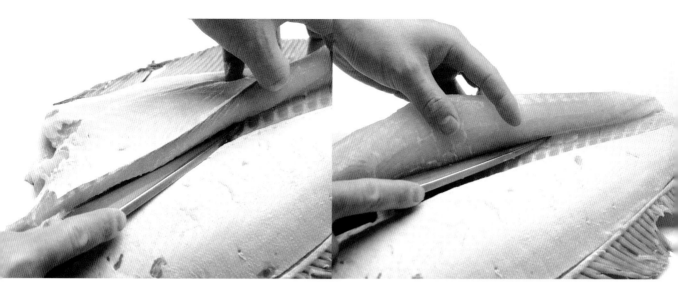

3 Turn the fish around so the tail is pointing diagonally up to the right. Hold the blade in a slanted position and cut from the center inwards along the middle bone, slicing a little at a time.

4 Make a cut with the tip of the blade between the fin and the body.

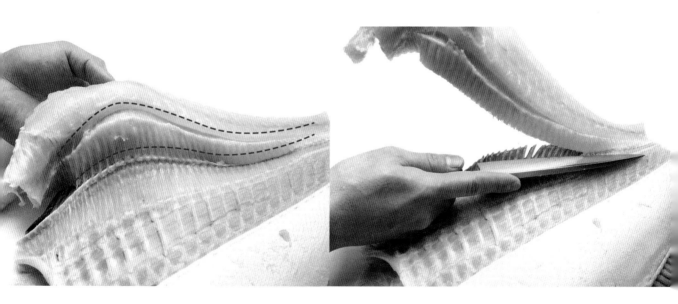

5 Lift up the body slowly. The part indicated with the red dashed line is the *engawa* or tail fin muscle.

6 Lay the blade flat against the fish, insert the blade between the fin and the body, and cut through slowly to remove the fillet from the bone.

7 Turn the fish around again so the head end is facing diagonally up to the right. Slant the blade and cut off the other side of the body from the bone, slicing through a little at a time. Remove the fillet slowly while moving the blade to cut.

8 Turn the fish over, and make a shallow cut along the edge of the fins on the other side around the body.

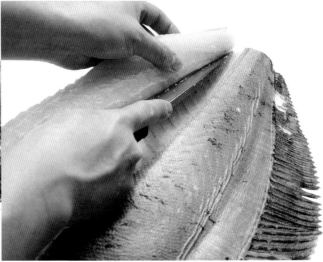

9 Turn the fish again so the tail end is facing diagonally up to the right. Hold down the fish lightly and make a middle cut through the fish over the backbone.

10 With the tail end facing diagonally up to the right, slant the blade and slowly cut through to the inner bones from the middle line inwards.

11 Keep cutting through to the center bones, and make a cut in between the fin and the body.

12 Lift up the body slowly. Lay the blade flat, and insert it in between the fin and the body as you slowly remove the fillet. Turn the blade around to face the head side to finish cutting.

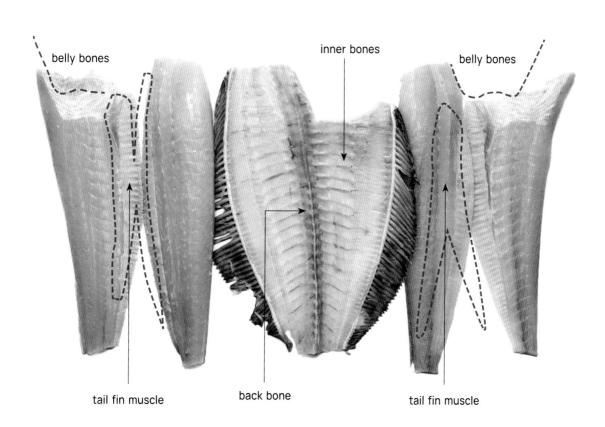

belly bones

inner bones

belly bones

tail fin muscle

back bone

tail fin muscle

The five-part fillet, consisting of two belly side fillets, two back side fillets, and the bones. After this is complete, the belly bones are removed and the skin is peeled off before the fillet is cut into *saku* blocks. The *engawa* tail fin muscle is also cut off and peeled.

Curing Fish Using Kombu (Kelp)

The term *kombu-jime* refers to a method of curing fillets or a block of fish between pieces of dried kombu seaweed. This method is often used with white fish such as sea bream and flounder. Kombu seaweed is packed with an umami substance called glutamic acid, which is transferred to the fish during the curing process. The fish has another source of umami called inosinic acid, and when combined with the glutamic acid, umami is increased several times over. This is called the compound effect of umami, and the kombu-jime method is a way of achieving this. In addition, as moisture in the fish is transferred to the dry kombu seaweed, the flesh of the fish firms up and the umami elements become concentrated, further enhancing the flavor.

The length of time fish is cured using the kombu-jime method varies from a few hours to several days. The taste and texture of the fish depend on how long it's cured for, and on factors such as temperature and humidity, so anticipation of the results is an enjoyable feature of the kombu-jime process, and those results really depend on the instincts of the chef.

Before curing

The top photo, below, shows a *saku*, or block, of olive flounder (*hirame*) before kombu-jime curing. Flounder used for this purpose is patted dry beforehand with a well-wrung-out kitchen cloth.

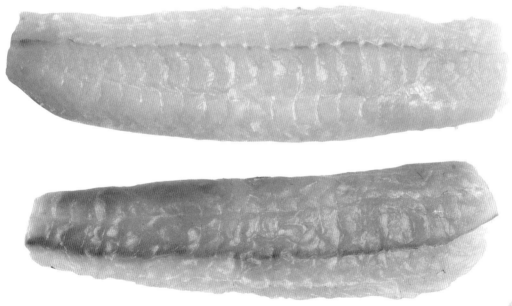

IMP + Glu
Stronger UMAMI

After curing

The bottom photo, above, shows a *saku*, or block, of olive flounder (*hirame*) after it has been cured between pieces of kombu seaweed for two days. The moisture has been absorbed by the kombu seaweed and the fish is firmer. It has also taken on a caramel color from the kombu. The combination of the inosinic acid (IMP) of the fish and the glutamic acid (Glu) of the kombu results in a very strong umami.

The Muscles of a Fish

For all fish, the muscles can be divided into two large groups: the striated muscles, and the smooth muscles. Invertebrates such as squid and octopus have obliquely striated muscles in addition to these.

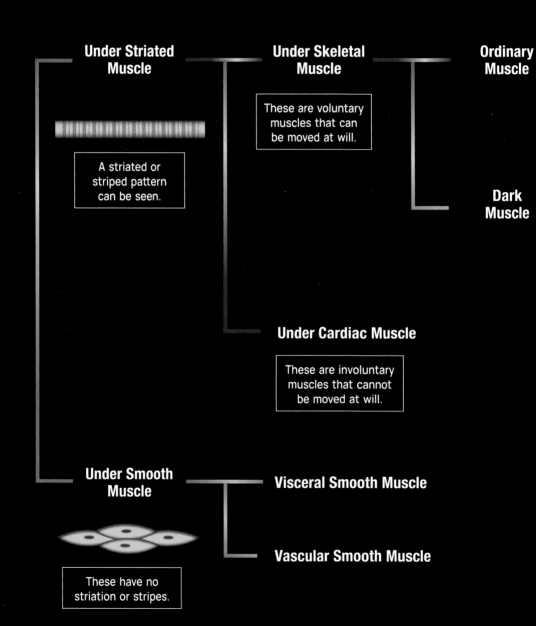

Under Striated Muscle

A striated or striped pattern can be seen.

Under Skeletal Muscle

These are voluntary muscles that can be moved at will.

Ordinary Muscle

Dark Muscle

Under Cardiac Muscle

These are involuntary muscles that cannot be moved at will.

Under Smooth Muscle

These have no striation or stripes.

Visceral Smooth Muscle

Vascular Smooth Muscle

White fish: White fish with texture should be sliced thinly on the diagonal to make it easier to chew.

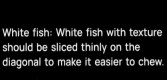

Amount of collagen

High

Low

White Muscle White Fish

The muscles of white fish don't bring in oxygen, but rather break down the glycogen in the muscles and produce energy that way. This allows for quick, sudden movement, which is useful when escaping predators.

Red Muscle Red Fish

The muscles of red fish are used by bringing in oxygen using myoglobin, a colored protein, and efficiently burning fat to produce energy. This allows the fish to swim for long periods.

Red fish: Soft red fish is sliced rather thickly by drawing the knife towards you.

Amount of dark red flesh in types of fish

Low   High

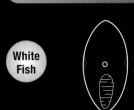 White Fish

 Red Fish

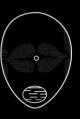

Fish with white flesh such as sea bream and flounder have small amounts of undeveloped dark red flesh.

Fish such as mackerel and horse mackerel have light red flesh, with dark red flesh inside.

Tuna has well-developed dark red flesh that reaches well inside the fish.

The Texture of Fish

The part of the fish that is eaten as a sushi topping is the muscle. Written like that it may not seem very appetizing, but whether the fish is cut with the grain, against the grain, or is tenderized, everything is related to how the muscles are handled. Most muscles used in sushi toppings are the skeletal muscles of the striated type (see chart on page 44). Although this also includes the dark red blood-rich muscles called *chiai*, this part is not used for sushi.

Biologically speaking, muscles are bundles of muscle fibers, and muscle fibers are bundles of myofibrils. The structure of the muscles differs by fish or seafood type, with each having its unique characteristics. By changing the structure of the muscles, the texture in particular is especially effected. If the muscle fibers become weakened or severed the texture will become soft, and if they shrink the texture will become tough.

White fish and red fish

Between the myofibrils, there's a water-soluble, spherical protein called sarcoplasm. This acts like the beads in a microbead cushion. White fish tend to have little sarcoplasm, while red fish usually have a lot of it.

Because there is little sarcoplasm to move against the pressure of the teeth when the muscle is chewed in a white fish, it feels tougher, while a red fish feels tender and soft because it has a lot of sarcoplasm. Of course this is just one reason for the differences in texture. The amount of water and fat in the flesh also makes a difference.

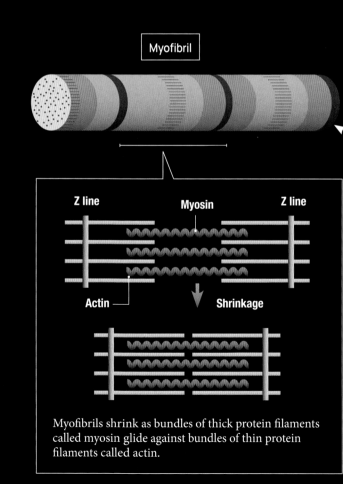

Myofibrils shrink as bundles of thick protein filaments called myosin glide against bundles of thin protein filaments called actin.

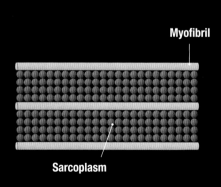

Myofibril

Sarcoplasm

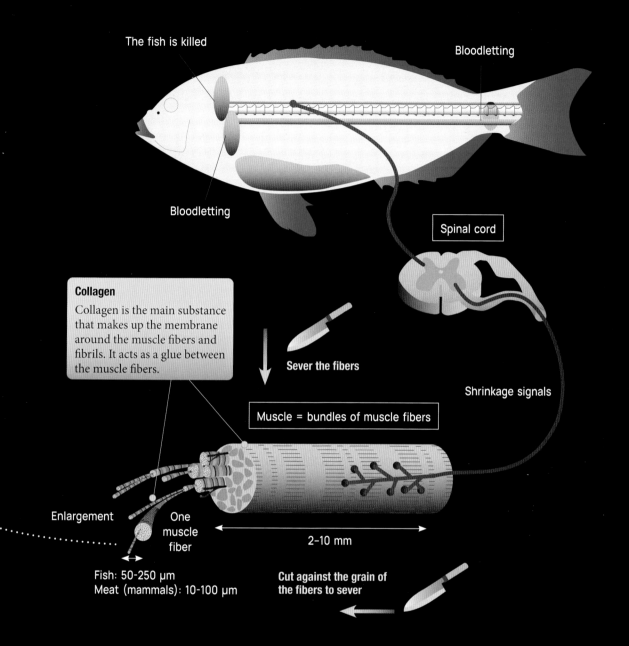

The fish is killed

Bloodletting

Bloodletting

Spinal cord

Collagen
Collagen is the main substance that makes up the membrane around the muscle fibers and fibrils. It acts as a glue between the muscle fibers.

Sever the fibers

Shrinkage signals

Muscle = bundles of muscle fibers

Enlargement

One muscle fiber

2–10 mm

Fish: 50-250 μm
Meat (mammals): 10-100 μm

Cut against the grain of the fibers to sever

How a fish becomes tender

After a fish is killed, it temporarily becomes tough and then becomes tender. It's thought there are two main reasons for this. One is because the myofibrils weaken. Myofibrils shrink because of protein filaments called myosin and actin gliding against each other (see diagram on the left). Filaments called Z-lines divide the stacked myosin and actin. After the fish is killed, the Z-lines become brittle and the myofibrils are weakened.

The other reason is the collagen; when a fish is killed, the collagen in it becomes brittle. Since collagen acts as a glue between muscle fibers, the whole muscle structure becomes loose. This looseness is what leads to the muscles becoming tender.

The Ikejime Method of Killing Fish

The term ikejime refers to the instant killing of fish after catching. Fish that are killed instantly remain fresh and tender for longer than fish that are allowed to die naturally after they have been caught.

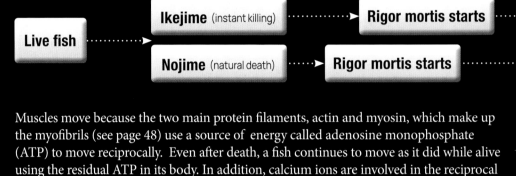

Fish

Muscles move because the two main protein filaments, actin and myosin, which make up the myofibrils (see page 48) use a source of energy called adenosine monophosphate (ATP) to move reciprocally. Even after death, a fish continues to move as it did while alive using the residual ATP in its body. In addition, calcium ions are involved in the reciprocal movement between the actin and myosin filaments; the amount of those calcium ions increases after the fish is killed. When a fish is killed instantly using the *ikejime* method (see page 28) the fish no longer moves, so the ATP in its body is not used. In other words, since there is plenty of ATP left in its muscles, the rigor mortis that occurs due to the loss of ATP occurs slowly. When a fish is allowed to die naturally (*nojime*), it continues to flop around. As it moves the ATP is used up, so rigor mortis sets in quickly.

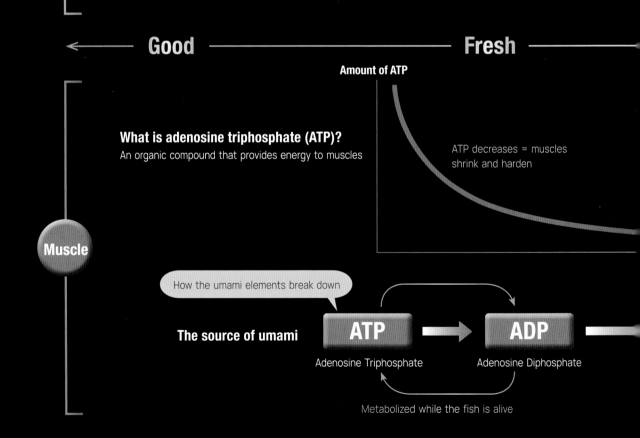

$\leftarrow$ **Good** —————————————— **Fresh** ——

Amount of ATP

What is adenosine triphosphate (ATP)?
An organic compound that provides energy to muscles

ATP decreases = muscles shrink and harden

Muscle

How the umami elements break down

The source of umami

ATP → **ADP**

Adenosine Triphosphate   Adenosine Diphosphate

Metabolized while the fish is alive

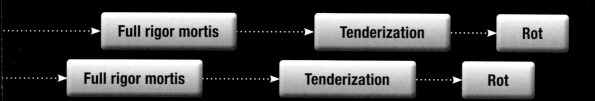

Full rigor mortis		Tenderization		Rot
Full rigor mortis		Tenderization		Rot

When the ATP in the body is depleted and the amount of calcium increases, the reciprocal movement between the actin and myosin stops. When this happens, they become stuck together. This is full rigor mortis.

After rigor mortis, the flesh becomes tender. This occurs because the muscle structure starts to break down. Since this structure is continuously stretched during rigor mortis, it becomes brittle. In addition tenderization is thought to occur because the adherence between the actin and myosin filaments becomes loosened. The aging process is the skillful manipulation of this reaction.

Bad ⟶

Formula for indicating the freshness of fish: the K value

$$K \text{ value (\%)} = \frac{HxR+Hx}{ATP+ADP+AMP+IMP+HxR+Hx} \times 100$$

The more time passes, the higher the K value gets.
It rises faster in red fish, and more slowly in white fish.

The lower the value, the fresher the fish. A fresh fish has a value of 10 to 30%. Sashimi has a value of less than 20%.

Time

Umami elements

AMP	IMP	HxR	Hx
Adenosine Monophosphate	Inosine Monophosphate	Inosine	Hypoxanthine

赤身

Red-fleshed Fish
(*Akami*)

Red-fleshed Fish

Fish with red flesh and a large amount of the dark, blood-rich muscles called *chiai* is known as *akami* in Japanese (note: the word *akami* is also used in this book to refer specifically to lean tuna). The contrast between bright red flesh and snow-white sushi rice is striking. Red-fleshed fish is high in fat content, giving a rich, distinctive flavor, and when it's put in the mouth there is a faint, fleeting taste of blood.

The main types of red-fleshed fish served at traditional Tokyo-style sushi restaurants are tuna (*maguro*) and skipjack tuna or bonito (*katsuo*). *Maguro* tuna is one of the most popular and expensive sushi toppings. However, up until the late 1940s it was treated as a low-class fish that was too high in fat. In fact, the fat content in the flesh of a tuna is as high as that of marbled beef. Because this fat does not coagulate even at low temperatures, it melts in the mouth. The Japanese name for the high-fat parts of the tuna, *toro*, comes from an ideophonic word that means melting or melty: *torori*.

Skipjack tuna has two seasons—early summer and the fall. During the former it's called "first katsuo," and during the latter it's called "returning katsuo," and returning katsuo has twelve times the fat content of first katsuo. Both maguro tuna and skipjack tuna are migratory fish that swim in the Kuroshio ocean current around Japan at tremendous speeds. Their bodies contain an abundance of the organic compound called ATP that provides energy to the muscles (see page 52). Not only is this ATP converted into the umami substance called inosinic acid, it combines with creatine, another substance in the muscles, as well as with an amino acid called histidine, to create a deep flavor unique to red fish.

All About Tuna

The tuna that is delivered to a sushi restaurant has already been broken down by the whole-saler after the early morning auction, first into four quarters on the back and belly sides, then these are then further cut into three parts — the head side (the *kami*), the mid section (the *naka*) and the tail end (the *shimo*), for a total of twelve pieces. These are then cut further into the size the individual restaurant wants. The flavor differs depending on the part of the fish, and of course the price differs too. The photo here shows a block called the "belly shimo," which is high in fat. This is then cut into the blocks used for sushi and sashimi called *saku*.

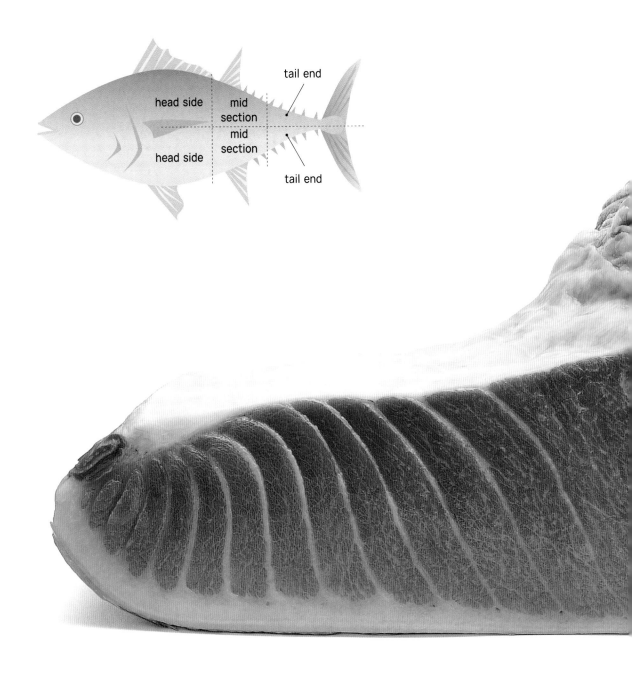

tail end

head side | mid section

mid section | head side

tail end

Tuna (*Maguro*)

There are several types of tuna, such as Pacific bluefin, Southern bluefin, albacore , bigeye and yellowfin, but the one called *maguro* or *hon-maguro* ("real tuna") in Japanese is usually Pacific bluefin tuna. It is so popular that the high prices the first auction of the year fetches are always news, and its 10 foot (3 meter) long body that can weigh up to 880 pounds (400 kilograms) makes it worthy of being called the king of tuna. It is characterized by a slightly acidic flavor, a refreshing taste of blood, rich umami and meltingly delicious fat. Most sushi restaurants age their tuna, and this aging process is extremely important. If the tuna is too fresh, although it has a strong texture and flavor, the umami can be lacking. But if it's aged for too long, although the umami becomes very strong, the other flavors and texture deteriorate. It's important to gauge the right timing to eat the fish and to not let it pass its peak.

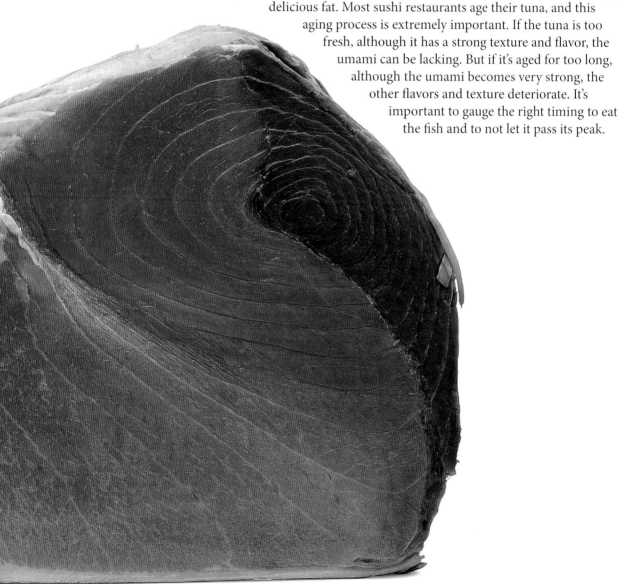

Filleting Tuna and Cutting It into Blocks

Unlike other fish used as sushi toppings, tuna is hardly ever brought into a restaurant whole. After the large pieces of fish described on the previous page are brought in, it's cut into blocks called *saku*.

To start with, one large piece is divided into four parts consisting of the blood-rich *chiai*, the lean *akami*, the medium-fat *chutoro* and the high-fat *otoro*. The chiai is the very dark red-black part. It's the muscle that runs vertically down the center of a fish, and has its dark color because it contains a large amount of a colored protein called myoglobin, which is related to hemoglobin. This muscle is used when the fish swims. Since myoglobin is contained in the muscle structure and provides oxygen, it is well developed in active fish such as tuna and skipjack tuna (*katsuo*). This part is hardly ever used for sushi. The remaining parts — the akami, chutoro and otoro — are cut to be used as sushi toppings.

1 The large block of tuna is placed so the dark red *chiai* is facing up. A *yanagiba* knife is inserted in between the chiai and the lean *akami* parts. The knife is pushed through following the dividing line between the parts, and the chiai is peeled off and removed.

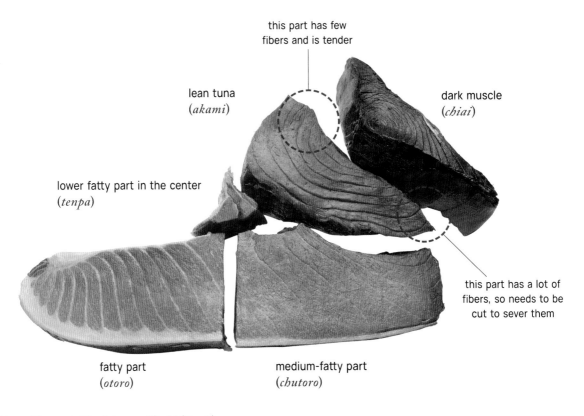

this part has few fibers and is tender

lean tuna (*akami*)

dark muscle (*chiai*)

lower fatty part in the center (*tenpa*)

this part has a lot of fibers, so needs to be cut to sever them

fatty part (*otoro*)

medium-fatty part (*chutoro*)

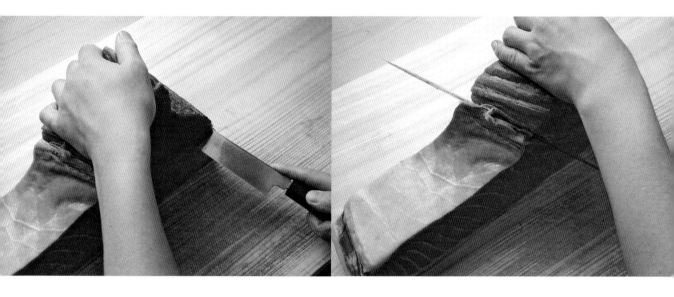

2 A cut is made parallel to the cutting board between the lean akami and the medium-fat *chutoro*, and sliced through.

3 The lean akami and the medium-fat chutoro are cut apart. The approximately 1 inch (3 cm) of lean meat at the top of the chutoro part is cut off. This part is called the *tenpa*.

4 The dark red chiai left on the lean akami part is removed cleanly.

5 The knife is inserted perpendicular to the cutting board, and the medium-fat chutoro and the high-fat *otoro* are divided.

When fish is used as a sushi topping, it is sliced as thinly as for sashimi. To facilitate this, the fish is cut into long rectangular blocks of a certain size, as shown in the photo on the right, and placed in the display case. Sometimes these blocks are sliced in front of the customer. When these display blocks are cut, the size of each slice that will be cut off to use as a sushi topping is considered. The length of the rectangular blocks differs depending on the chef, but in most cases it's about the length of the width of the four fingers of the hand held together.

中トロ

Medium-fatty part
(*Chutoro*)

With the skin still on it, the block of *chutoro* is sliced pieces about 1 inch (3 cm) wide with the knife held perpendicular to the cutting board. When the knife reaches the skin, rather than cutting through it, the knife is turned around so it's parallel to the cutting board, and the skin is sliced off. The peeled-off skin is held against the cut surface, wrapped in paper and stored. (The skin of *otoro* is handled in the same way.)

大トロ

Fatty Part
(*Otoro*)

1 With the skin still on it, the block of otoro is sliced into pieces about 1 inch (3 cm) wide, with the knife held perpendicular to the cutting board.

2 When the knife reaches the skin, rather than cutting through it, the knife is turned around so it's parallel to the cutting board, and the skin is sliced off. The rectangular blocks are trimmed to the same length.

赤身

Lean Tuna
(*Akami*)

1 The block is cut into approximately ½-inch (1.5-cm) wide pieces.

2 The rectangular blocks are trimmed to the same length.

Chutoro

Otoro

Akami

Comparing Red Fish and White Fish

Red Fish
(Akami)

Large amount of colored proteins

Migratory fish

High activity

Large amount of dark red *chiai* muscles

High amount of umami

Red muscles

Red fish are migratory fish whose muscles are characterized by their red color, a large amount of which is dark red muscle or *chiai*. Even if it's not really red, fish with red-tinged flesh is also considered to be in this category. The reason why the flesh of the fish turns red is because it contains a large amount of a colored protein called myoglobin. Colored proteins perform the function of carrying oxygen to the muscles. Since migratory fish swim at high speeds and are very active, they require oxygen. This is the reason why they contain a large amount of colored proteins and turn red. Also, they contain a higher amount of umami substances than white fish, as well as a higher amount of fat, which is why red fish tastes richer than white. However, it can smell fishier more easily, due to the oxidation of the fat and to decomposition.

Red fish refers to fish such as skipjack tuna, tuna, mackerel, Pacific saury, sardines and so on.

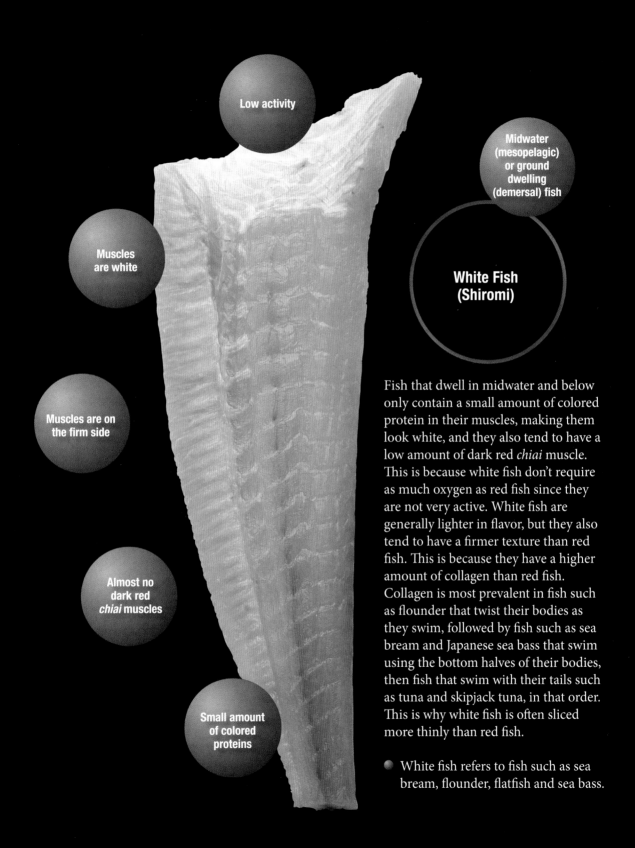

Low activity

Muscles are white

Muscles are on the firm side

Almost no dark red *chiai* muscles

Small amount of colored proteins

Midwater (mesopelagic) or ground dwelling (demersal) fish

White Fish (Shiromi)

Fish that dwell in midwater and below only contain a small amount of colored protein in their muscles, making them look white, and they also tend to have a low amount of dark red *chiai* muscle. This is because white fish don't require as much oxygen as red fish since they are not very active. White fish are generally lighter in flavor, but they also tend to have a firmer texture than red fish. This is because they have a higher amount of collagen than red fish. Collagen is most prevalent in fish such as flounder that twist their bodies as they swim, followed by fish such as sea bream and Japanese sea bass that swim using the bottom halves of their bodies, then fish that swim with their tails such as tuna and skipjack tuna, in that order. This is why white fish is often sliced more thinly than red fish.

● White fish refers to fish such as sea bream, flounder, flatfish and sea bass.

Aging Fish

Aging means to store fish or meat for a specific period of time at a low temperature in order to increase its flavor. It is mostly used for meat, but it is used for fish too. Unlike meat, fish start to get tender not very long after the end of rigor mortis. For sashimi, fish that is just killed is preferred because of its freshness, but fish that has been rested in the refrigerator is often used for sushi toppings. This is because when a fish has just been brought in, its texture may be too pronounced, and it often does not meld well with the sushi rice. The fish may also be further "aged" depending on the variety. This is especially true for tuna and flounder.

The aging process consists of cutting the fish into blocks, wrapping in paper towels or kitchen cloths, and refrigerating. How long the fish is aged for depends on the desired flavor, aroma and texture. It also depends on the amount of ATP (see facing page) in the fish and how much the proteins break down.

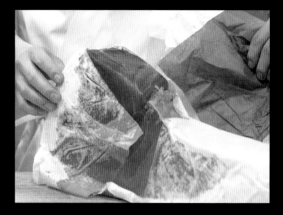

The fish is rested so that it reaches an ideal state for melding with the sushi rice.

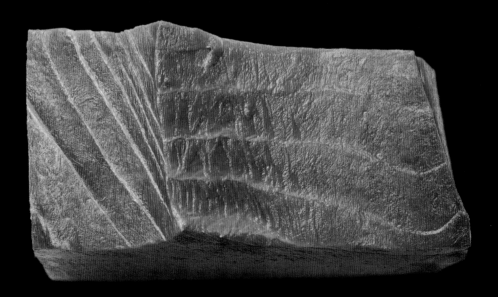

Aged tuna

Visualization of toughness and flavor, and ideal eating time

Tough **High**

Soft **Low**

Texture — Texture

Inosinic acid

Ideal time to eat

Inosinic acid

The fish is killed ——— Time ———→

From ATP to inosinic acid

When a fish is alive, it moves by using a substance called adenosine monophosphate (ATP) as the source of energy. When the fish dies, the ATP contained in the muscles breaks down due to enzymes, and during the process turns into a source of umami called inosinic acid (IMP). Inosinic acid breaks down further and turns into substances called inosine (HxR) and hypoxanthine (Hx). The reaction time from when ATP is transformed to IMP is very short, but the transformation from IMP into HxR occurs very slowly (see page 49). With aging it is important to gauge how much IMP transformed from ATP has accumulated, and how and when it starts to reduce, thus reducing the amount of umami.

Proteins to amino acids

When a fish is aged, the various enzymes in it work to change its condition. Proteins have a structure made up of chains of amino acids tangled together like chains of beads. Because the enzymes in the fish sever the connections between these chains of amino acid beads, a large amount of amino acids and peptides that affect the flavor of the fish are produced. Peptides have the effect of suppressing acidic flavors (which are considered undesirable in fish), and work to lessen this acidity as the fish ages. This is one of the reasons why the fish becomes tastier and more well-rounded in flavor. The collagen that makes the flesh of the fish firm is also broken down by enzymes, so the fish becomes more tender.

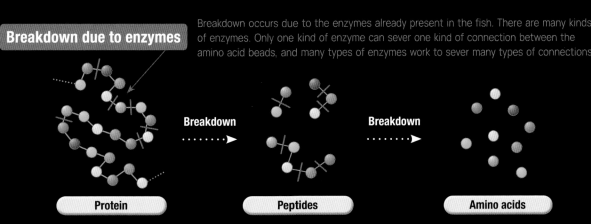

Breakdown due to enzymes

Breakdown occurs due to the enzymes already present in the fish. There are many kinds of enzymes. Only one kind of enzyme can sever one kind of connection between the amino acid beads, and many types of enzymes work to sever many types of connections

Breakdown ········▶

Breakdown ········▶

Protein

Peptides

Amino acids

Protein consists of lots of amino acids connected and entangled together.

Peptides are more than two amino acid beads connected together.

Protein is broken down into amino acids. Around twenty types of amino

Silver-skinned Fish

光りもの

Silver-skinned
Fish
(*Hikarimono*)

The term *hikarimono*, meaning "shiny fish" is unique to sushi restaurants. There are all kinds of silver-skinned fish, but hikarimono refers to fish that have a shiny surface. Hikarimono are marinated in vinegar or salt before they are used as sushi toppings. They have a different texture, aroma and flavor from raw fish, and the process of marinating the fish is the essence of what Edomae (traditional Tokyo-style) sushi is about.

At a sushi restaurant, hikarimono means fish such as gizzard shad (*kohada*), horse mackerel (*aji*), mackerel (*saba*), Japanese whiting (*kisu*), Japanese halfbeak or needlefish (*sayori*) and so on. The source of the shininess of the fish is a substance called guanine, which can be found as crystal shaped plates in the chromatophores (color-producing cells) on the surface of the scales. Although guanine is colorless it reflects light, which is why silver-skinned fish have a shiny appearance.

When nigirizushi first appeared during the Edo period, the small silver-skinned fish caught in Tokyo Bay were marinated in vinegar or salt or with kombu seaweed. Nowadays the fish is usually peeled, but back then it was eaten with the skin intact because it was very well marinated. The term hikarimono itself, meaning "things that shine," shows how stylish traditional Tokyo-style sushi is.

The taste and texture of the fish can differ greatly depending on how skilfully salt and vinegar are used with it. It's often said "you can see how good a sushi place is if you have their hikarimono."

Preparing Gizzard Shad

Gizzard shad (*kohada*) is a silver-skinned fish (see page 62) that becomes shinier when marinated in vinegar. It has a strong, distinctive flavor and aroma, thin flesh with many small bones, and a pleasant, slightly crunchy texture. The black spots on the surface of its blue-tinged skin are very beautiful, making this a sushi topping that is as nice to look at as it is to eat. Choose one with a plump body for the best sushi. The fish has serrated scales on its belly, so the preparation starts by removing these carefully with a knife.

Preparation steps

1 Leave the fish soaking in salt water until it's ready to be descaled. This causes the water to penetrate the spaces between the scales and makes them easier to remove.
2 Place the fish with the belly side facing you, hold it down with the middle and index fingers and cut off the back fin with a deba knife (see page 25).
3 Hold the knife on the fish, and scrape off the scales from the tail end going towards the head end.

4 Use the black spot near the head to mark the place where the head begins. Hold the blade perpendicular to the fish and cut off the head and tail.
5 Place the fish with the tail facing away from you, and cut off vertically the plump belly part that contains the innards.
6 Push the innards out with your thumb and rinse the fish in water.

鰶 Large Gizzard Shad (*Konoshiro*)

Shusseuo Shinko → Kohada → Konoshiro

What is a gizzard shad?

Gizzard shad is a fish from the herring family whose name in Japanese changes depending on its stage of development. Fish such as this are called *shusseuo,* which means "fish that advance in the world." Large gizzard shad are called *konoshiro,* and grow to around 10 to 12 inches (25 to 30 cm) long. In the Kanto region around Tokyo, gizzard shad that are around 2½ to 4 inches (7 to 10 cm) long are called *kohada* (in the Kansai region around Osaka and Kyoto they're called *tsunashi*), and smaller ones are called *shinko.* Very small gizzard shad or shinko are sold at high prices; several are used for one piece of sushi and enjoyed as "multi-layer marinades."

1 Place the fish with the head side facing to the right and the tail end to the left. Hold the fish down lightly, hold the knife parallel to the cutting board, and insert the knife along the inner bones.

2 Run the tip of the blade along the bones to cut along it. Make sure to run the knife right along the bones, so that the fillets on each side will have the same thickness.

3 Push open the fish while stroking along the back bone with your finger.

4 Place the fish skin side up. Insert the knife from the head side between the flesh and the bone, and remove the bone. Be careful not to leave any flesh on the bone, and to remove only the bone as you cut.

5 Place the fish skin side down with the tail end facing away from you. Shave off the belly bones, holding the blade against the flesh.

6 Take the bones off the other side in the same way as in Step 5 while flipping the blade over (this is called an upside-down knife).

Curing Gizzard Shad with Vinegar and Salt

Vinegar-marinated gizzard shad is made by first salting it, and then marinating it in vinegar. After it has been taken out of the vinegar it is rested for a few hours up to a whole day to let the flavors settle down. The amount of salt and vinegar used and the time required for each step are finely gauged depending on the thickness of the flesh, how much fat is on it and so on. Large or thick fish or ones with a lot of fat are marinated for longer times, and of course the opposite is true for thinner, lean fish. It's necessary to make instant judgments on how the fish should be handled as soon as it's filleted, making this a fish that requires experience, good instincts and skill from the chef. That's why it's known as the grand champion of sushi toppings!

Before

After

Marinating gizzard shad in vinegar

1 Sprinkle salt on a flat sieve, and put the filleted gizzard shad on top of it.
2 With a handful of salt in your right hand, rotate the sieve with your left hand as you sprinkle the salt on the fillets generously.
3 Leave to rest for a while then rinse under running water. Put the fillets back on the sieve to drain off.

4 Put the fillets in vinegar, and stir around well to rinse them.
5 Put the fillets back onto the sieve to drain off the vinegar. Put fresh vinegar in a container and marinate the fillets for 5 to 10 minutes.
6 Drain off the vinegar again, and put the fish into a container to rest.

Salted

Washed with Vinegar

Fresh raw fish has a pH value that is slightly on the acid side of neutral. The pH drops due to the lactic acid produced by rigor mortis, and rises back up to its original level as rigor mortis ends. Fish that are marinated in vinegar include gizzard shad, mackerel and horse mackerel, which are considered as fish that go off fast. As they lose freshness, they produce an odiferous substance called trimethylamine, which causes a "fishy" smell. Trimethylamine is alkaline, so the fishy smell can be suppressed by combining the fish with acidic vinegar and thus changing the pH value.

Fish is salted to give it a salty flavor of course, but the real reason is to change the nature of the proteins in the flesh. The myofibrils that make up 50 percent of the proteins in fish flesh (see page 46) dissolve in around 2 to 6 percent saline solution. When fish is salted and left to rest, the moisture near the surface of the fish is drawn out because of the salt's dehydrating properties. This means the fish becomes coated with a high-concentrate saline solution, which transforms the proteins into a soft, jellylike state. But if the fish is left to salt for too long, the concentration of the saline solution will keep rising. When it reaches around 15 percent the jellification of the proteins stops but the dehydration process continues, turning the fish tough and unpleasant to eat.

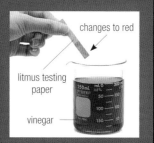
Washed and marinated with vinegar

Washed and Marinated with Vinegar

When vinegar, which can be called "the soul of protein" is added to fish, the proteins are denatured (see introduction, facing page). Muscles are made up of many cells, some that dissolve in water. The pH of fresh raw fish is around 6, but when it is put into vinegar and the pH becomes more acid (around pH 5) the gaps between the myofibrils decrease because of the vinegar, tightening the flesh. As the pH continues to drop below 4, the myofibril protein starts to dissolve in the acid, so the flesh becomes soft and mushy. But if the fish is salted and tightened before putting it in vinegar, the myofibrils do not dissolve and remain intact, so the flesh continues to tighten. This is why vinegar-marinated fish looks white.

Why salting is necessary for vinegar marinading

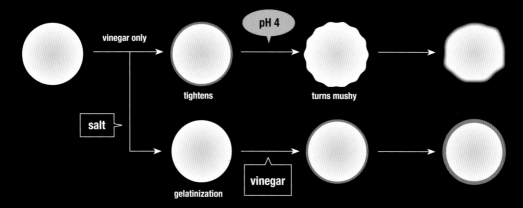

vinegar only

pH 4

tightens

turns mushy

salt

gelatinization

vinegar

青
魚

Blue-skinned
Fish
(*Aozakana*)

Blue-skinned Fish

This term refers to fish with a bluish tinge to their bodies, such as horse mackerel (*aji*), Pacific saury (*sanma*) and sardine (*iwashi*).

Blue-skinned fish have red muscles because they are very active; in addition they have well-developed blood-rich dark red muscle (*chiai*), so if they had to be categorized as white or red fish they'd belong in the red fish category. They have a large amount of flavor essences that give each type of fish a unique taste and aroma. Blue-skinned fish that is in season and high in fat is especially popular, so Pacific saury or mackerel in the fall and horse mackerel in the summer are looked forward to every year. Blue-skinned fish deteriorate rapidly and go bad easily, so until recently they were usually marinated in vinegar, but nowadays, thanks to advances in distribution methods, they can be eaten raw too.

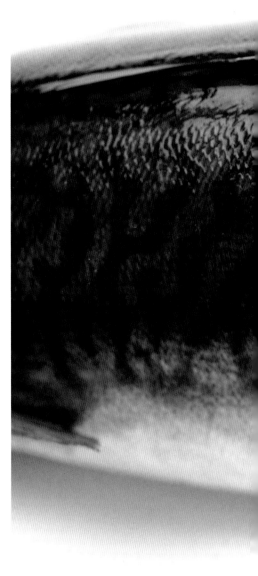

鯖

Mackerel (*Saba*)

There are two types of mackerel that are both called *saba* in Japanese: blue mackerel (Scomber australasicus) and chub mackerel (Scomber japonicus). The photograph shows a chub mackerel, characterized by the boomerang-shaped markings on its body. Mackerel is most often salted and marinated in vinegar, and when this process is carried out carefully, the flesh has a tender, melting texture with a distinctive taste. Some people are allergic to the mackerel family and may break out in a rash. This is an adverse reaction to the large amount of histamine that accumulates within the muscles when the mackerel dies.

Filleting a Blue-skinned Fish into Three

Blue-skinned fish are cut apart into three pieces — the upper body, the lower body and the bones — and the upper and lower body parts become the *saku* block used for sushi toppings. Before the fish is filleted, the pre-filleting procedure called *mizu arai*, or water-washing, is performed, which involves removing the scales, removing and washing out the innards and cutting off the head and tail (see page 32).

1 Cut off the upper half of the body. Place the fish on the cutting board with the belly facing you and the tail to the left. Hold the upper body open lightly, insert the knife along the inner bone, and cut through towards the tail.

2 Turn the fish around so the tail is facing to the right. Insert the knife from the back along the fin, and cut through along the inner bone towards the head end.

3 When the knife reaches the head end, take it out and turn it around so the blade is facing the tail. Insert the knife and cut towards the tail, removing the upper body half. Repeat on the other side.

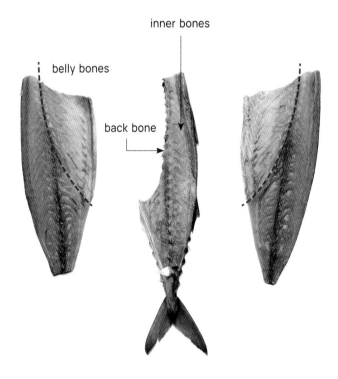

inner bones

belly bones

back bone

A fish filleted into three pieces — the upper body, the inner bones and the lower body. The belly bones are removed to create the *saku*, the block of flesh that is used for sashimi and sushi.

Keeping Sardines Fresh

Why is it said that sardines and horse mackerel go bad fast?

In the long history of sushi that goes back to the Edo period (1603–1868), sardines are a relatively new sushi topping. The reason for this is that sardines (*iwashi*) go off very fast, so it was difficult to eat them raw before the advent of refrigeration.

There are several reasons why sardines and horse mackerel (*aji*) deteriorate rapidly. For one thing, sardines are caught in large quantities in fishing nets, rarely one at a time. Therefore it's impossible to kill them instantly with the *ikejime* method (see page 28). Their blood is also not removed. This means the fish go through a lot of stress before they die, using up a lot of ATP, an organic compound that is a source of umami (see page 61).

In addition, sardines have very tender flesh that goes bad quickly and is also high in fat. A compound called trimethylamine is produced—the cause of fishy odors—due to the effect of enzymes on the surface of the decomposing parts. Also the fat becomes oxidized and deteriorates, which also leads to a bad smell. Sardines must be put into ice water as soon as they are brought in, and the innards must be removed and washed out. Since they are so tender, they must be treated with care so that the flesh is not damaged, and turned into sushi toppings quickly.

What's behind that fishy smell?

bacteria and enzymes

no odor	the cause of odors
trimethylamine N-oxide	trimethylamine

* Alkaline
* Turns into an acid substance with no odor = eliminating odors

Odor-causing trimethylamine (TMA) starts out as trimethylamine N-oxide (TMAO), which has no odor. TMAO is introduced into the fish via what it feeds on. After death, the micro-organisms and enzymes on the surface of the fish work to create TMA, which leads to that "fishy" odor. Because freshwater fish do not have TMAO, they don't have the typical odor that is present in seawater fish.

Washing and Curing Fish

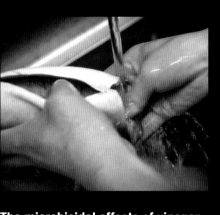

Washing the fish

Fish should be washed with fresh water. This is not only for cosmetic purposes such as rinsing off the blood, or to make it easier to handle afterwards, but is important in order to wash off the odor-causing trimethylamine (TMA, see page 73) that coats the fish around its innards and suppress any smelliness. In addition, the main cause of food poisoning from fish and seafood is a bacterium called *Vibrio parahaemolyticus*. This bacterium likes salt-water conditions, and is weak in fresh water. So when washing a fish, use fresh water not salt water.

The microbicidal effects of vinegar

Vinegar has been known to have disinfectant or microbidical effects since ancient times. Vinegar contains acetic acid, which is very acidic (around pH 3). The bacteria that cause food poisoning cannot live in acidic conditions, so if an acid substance is poured over them it helps to disinfect them, or prevent the proliferation of such bacteria.

A 2.5% dilution vinegar is a disinfectant against most if not all bacteria, and when it's used in conjunction with salt it is said to be even more effective. In other words sushi vinegar, which is a mixture of salt and vinegar, aids in disinfecting fish. In addition, molds prefer a pH of around 5, so the combination of salt and vinegar is useful in suppressing their growth too.

The microbicidal effects of vinegar with added sugar and salt

Name of bacterium	Time needed to disinfect in minutes - at 86°F (30°C)			
	Vinegar	Sushi vinegar mixture		
		Sweet vinegar	Salty vinegar	Sweet and salty vinegar
E. coli	30	30	10	10
Citrobacter freundii	10	30	5	10
Salmonella	10	10	5	10
Morganella morganii	10	30	5	10
Staphylococcus aureus	10	30	10	10
Vibrio parahaemolyticus	<0.25	<0.25	<0.25	<0.25

Microbicidal Effects of Vinegar, Journal of Food Science and Technology, July 28, 1981. Etsuzo Entani et. al.

The above chart shows the microbicidal effects of 2.5% dilution vinegar mixed with sugar (10%) or salt (3.5%), or both. The three types of sushi vinegar mixture shown above are known in Japanese as *amasu*, *nihaizu* and *sanbaizu* respectively. The numbers show the amount of time in minutes it takes to disinfect; the lower the number, the more effective it is as a disinfectant. Although the vinegar and sugar mixture is less effective as a disinfectant than vinegar alone, the effect is strengthened with vinegar + salt (*nihaizu*), while vinegar + salt + sugar (*sanbaizu*) lies between vinegar + sugar and vinegar + salt in effectiveness. This shows that the mixture of vinegar and salt often used to flavor sushi rice is a good disinfectant, or in other words has a high microbicidal effect.

Fermenting *funazushi*. It is made using a type of funa (crucian carp) called *gengorobuna* or *nigorobuna*.

Photo credit: Funazushi Uoji, Shiga Prefecture

The Lactic Acid Fermentation Effect of Funazushi

It's believed that sushi originated with *narezushi* or fermented sushi (see page 7). The *nare* part of the word means "to mature," and the most famous example of matured sushi in Japan is *funazushi*, a dish where fish and rice are fermented together. The rice is discarded and only the fish is eaten. It was originally a way to preserve fish, and requires a long time to ferment.

While the fish is curing, its muscles break down and a variety of umami substances occur. At the same time organic acids such as lactic acid and alcohol are produced due to the increase in lactobacilli or lactic acid bacteria. These organic acids lower the pH of the fish, suppressing the growth of micro-organisms and preserving the fish.

The initial salting process uses a saline water solution that's as high as 15%, so the growth of food poisoning causing bacteria such as *Clostridium botulinum* is also suppressed. It's said that *Clostridium botulinum* cannot proliferate in a salt concentration higher than 5%.

The bacterium *Vibrio parahaemolyticus* can cause gastroenteritis or stomach flu. It occurs almost exclusively in fish and seafood and related processed-food products. It can also be transmitted via equipment or water that has been in contact with affected fish or seafood. It prefers a salty environment, and grows most vigorously in a salt concentration that's the same as sea water, around 3 percent. If conditions are right it divides and proliferates in 8 to 9 minutes. It does not proliferate under 50°F (10°C). It cannot live in heat, and if it's boiled it is killed instantly. (Source: National Institute of Infectious Diseases website.)

The bacterium *Clostridium botulinum* which causes food poisoning thrives in low oxygen conditions. It does not occur if the pH is under 4.6. When rice ferments its pH drops to around 4 to 4.5, so *Clostridium botulinum* does not occur.

Curing Fish with Sugar

The reason why the flesh of a fish firms up when salt is sprinkled on it is because its surface is covered with a semipermeable membrane. This allows water to pass through, but not salt. When salt is sprinkled onto fish the salt content of the cells near the surface increases, so the moisture in the fish is drawn out, causing dehydration. Since the water-soluble elements that are the cause of fishy odors are also drawn out, this suppresses any unpleasant smells.

This effect can be seen with sugar also. Since curing a fish in salt makes it salty and tough, sometimes sugar is used to cure mackerel instead of salt. Another method of curing fish is to sugar it first, and then to salt it.

How Dehydration Works

Cells are covered on both sides with a semipermeable membrane. This is a membrane with very small holes, through which only water can pass. Substances like sugar or umami elements with large molecules cannot penetrate it. When liquids with different concentrations are divided by a semipermeable membrane, the water in the low-concentration solution tries to pass through to the higher concentration side to thin it out.

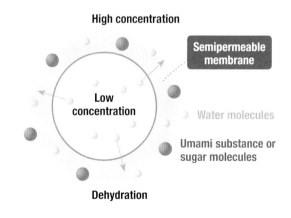

High concentration

Semipermeable membrane

Low concentration

Water molecules

Umami substance or sugar molecules

Dehydration

Shellfish
(*Kai*)

Shellfish

In the Edo period (1603–1868), Tokyo Bay was rich with shellfish. For this reason, it has been used as a sushi topping since those times. However, back then, instead of being eaten raw it was simmered or marinated in vinegar. Nowadays, several varieties of shellfish are used raw as sushi toppings. The peak season for most of these is in the cold months up until the spring, and their colorful presence graces display cases during the winter.

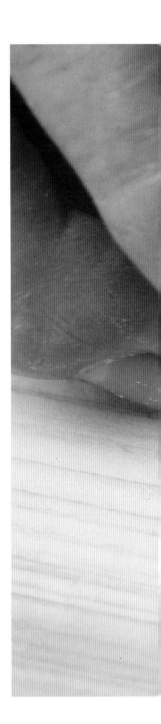

The shellfish used as sushi toppings are gaper clam (*mirugai*, Tresus keenae), ark clam or red clam (*akagai*, Anadara broughtonii), egg cockle (*torigai*, Fulvia mutica), abalone (*awabi*, Haliotis), Japanese scallop (*hotategai*, Mizuhopecten yessoensis), Asian hard clam (*hamaguri*, Meretrix lusoria), razor clam (*tairagai*, Atrina pectinata), surf clam (*aoyagi*, Mactra chinensis), multicolored abalone (*tokobushi*, Sulculus diversicolor supertexta), surf clam scallop (*kobashira*, from Mactra chinensis) and so on. Of these, abalone, Asian hard clam and multicolored abalone are called *nimono,* or simmered items, and require the skills to cook them until they are just the right texture to match up with sushi rice.

The appeal of raw shellfish is its springy, chewy texture, the refreshing flavor of the sea, the intense umami and a unique sweetness. The texture is thanks to the abundance of collagen; the taste is thanks to amino acids such as glycine and glutamic acid, organic acids such as succinic acid, and glycogen. The flavorful "essence" of the shellfish is very much affected by its freshness. Even if live shellfish still in their shells are brought in, care must be taken to maintain their freshness after they are taken out of the shells.

Texture Comes from Collagen

The texture of shellfish is related to the amount of collagen between the muscles. The larger the amount of collagen the firmer the shellfish, and when there's just a small amount it is said to be on the soft side. The chart below shows the amount of collagen in different types of fish and shellfish. Ones that can be eaten raw have less than 3% collagen, but octopus and abalone contain more than 8%. Collagen-rich items take on a characteristic tenderness when they are cooked.

The amount of collagen in fish and seafood muscles (% of the amount of muscle)			
Sardine	2	Squid or cuttlefish	2–3
Sea bream	3	Octopus	6
Skipjack tuna	2	Abalone	5–40 (depending on the part)

Preparing Gaper Clams

What is a gaper clam?

In Japanese the gaper clam is widely called *mirugai*. Its formal Japanese name is *mirukui* and its biological name is Tresus keenae. With its rich flavor of the sea and strong umami, as well as its thick, springy texture, it is a very popular sushi topping. The part used as a sushi topping is the siphon, which takes in and releases sea water. It is long and thick and often sticks out of the shell. The reason why the siphon is black is because a kelp called *miru* is stuck to it. It's said that it got the name *mirukui*, which means "miru eater," because it looks like the shellfish is eating this miru. Gaper clam is in season from the fall to the spring. It has become scarce in recent years and is therefore expensive to use as a sushi topping, so the shellfish called geoduck (*namigai* in Japanese, Panopea generosa) which also has a big siphon, is often substituted. But even geoduck is becoming scarcer these days.

Opening the shell

1 Insert a shelling knife or a deba knife (see page 25) in between the two closed shells, and cut as you gouge out the adductor muscle. One side will come off right away.

2 Cut the adductor muscle that is stuck to the other side of the shell.

3 Pull on the siphon to separate the body from the shell. Rinse well in water.

Preparing the clam

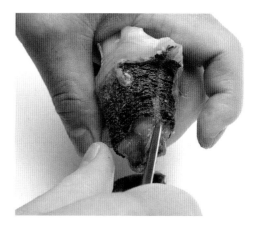

1 The gaper clam can be divided into the siphon and the tongue. Insert the knife as shown in the photograph, and keep the adductor muscle attached to the siphon while prying it off the tongue. The tongue is not used as a sushi topping.

2 The black substance on the siphon is kelp. Scrape this off. Make a cut in the tough beak-like part.

A rinsed and prepared gaper clam. The black substance that's scraped off is kelp.

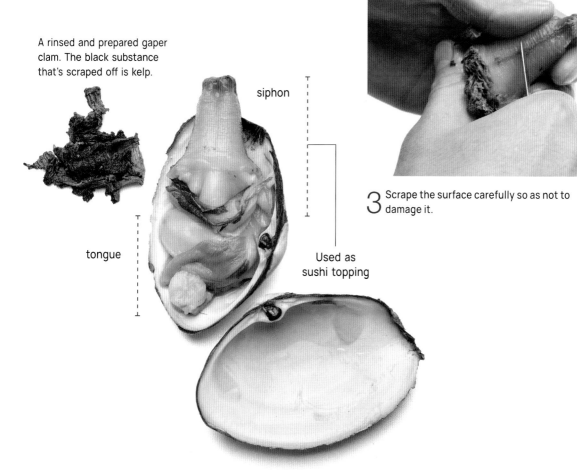

3 Scrape the surface carefully so as not to damage it.

siphon

tongue

Used as sushi topping

Opening up the siphon meat

1 Hold the knife parallel to the cutting board and cut halfway through the siphon. Continue to cut until you are almost all the way through.

2 Hold the meat down with the knife as you butterfly it open. Peel off the membrane stuck to the surface. Cut off the tip. The clam often has sand on it, which needs to be rinsed off well.

Gaper clam ready to be used as a sushi topping.
It's cut to emphasize the pointed, colored parts.

The Muscles of a Shellfish

The muscles of a fish can be divided into striated and smooth types (see page 44), but shellfish, squid or cuttlefish and octopuses also have oblique muscles. Shellfish always have their shells closed in the sea, which is why their muscles have a unique texture.

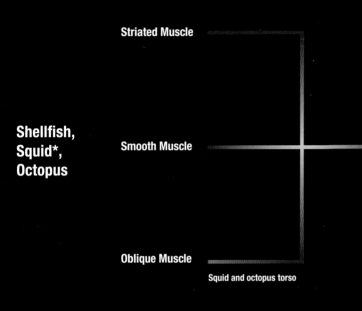

Striated Muscle

Shellfish, Squid*, Octopus

Smooth Muscle

Oblique Muscle

Squid and octopus torso

*See more information on page 98

Scallops

The muscles of scallops such as the Asian hard clam are called adductor muscles, which consist of striated and smooth muscles. The striated muscles are used to quickly close up the shell, and the smooth muscles are used to keep the shell closed. In other words if there are a lot of smooth muscles this creates strength, and it's hard to open up the shell.

Live shellfish have closed shells, and no matter what you do it's not easy to open them. The force with which the shells are kept closed is said to be around 0.155 square inch (1 sq. cm) per 220 pounds (100 kg). This is why the only way to open up a live shellfish it to pry it open with a tool. However, if a shellfish is grilled or otherwise cooked, the structure of the smooth muscles changes and separates from the shell, which then opens up.

The color of blood in shellfish

All vertebrates, not just fish, use iron in their bodies to transport oxygen. The blood pigment that contains iron combined with oxygen is hemoglobin. Hemoglobin is red, which is why blood is red. Invertebrates such as shellfish, shrimp and squid or cuttlefish use copper to transport oxygen. The blood pigment that combines copper with oxygen, the equivalent of hemoglobin in vertebrates, is called hemocyanin. Because this has a dark blue or green color, the blood of these animals is dark blue or green. The ark or red clam (*akagai*) is an exception to this rule since it uses iron to transport oxygen in the same way as vertebrates, which is why it has bright red blood.

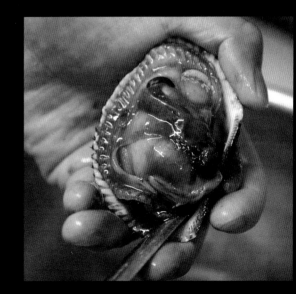

Preparing Ark Clams

Choose shells that feel full and packed when you hold them in your hand. Ark clams that weigh around 3½ to 4¼ ounces (100 to 120 g) are often used. They turn lean after the spring equinox since they carry eggs. Take care not to damage the inner flesh when you open up the shell with a knife.

What is an ark clam?

Also known as red clam, this shellfish gets it name because of its beautiful bright red color. It has a soft texture, and when fresh ones are opened up they fill the air with the fragrance of the sea. To turn them into sushi toppings they are partially cut through and slammed down on the cutting board. The muscles of a fresh ark clam respond to this treatment by shrinking up, causing the cut part to open up and the color to become even brighter. The mantle or "rope" of the ark clam is also used as a sushi topping separately, or in sushi rolls with cucumber.

Opening the shell

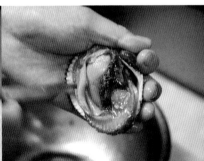

1 Hold the shell with the hinge facing up. Insert a shelling or deba knife (see page 25) in between the hinges and twist hard to separate them.

2 Run the knife along the edge of the shell as you turn the shell and remove the adductor muscle. One side of the shell will come off.

3 Separate the adductor muscle from the other side of the shell, and take out the body.

Preparing the clam

1 Insert the knife while pinching the plump part of the removed body with two fingers.

2 Run the knife along the top of the rope-like mantle, and cut the mantle off the body.

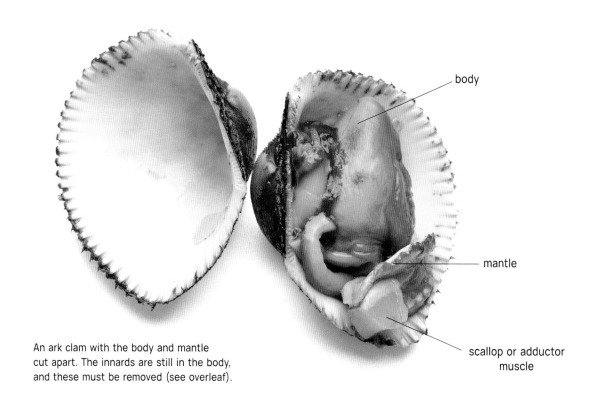

body

mantle

scallop or adductor muscle

An ark clam with the body and mantle cut apart. The innards are still in the body, and these must be removed (see overleaf).

Opening the body

1 Slice through center of the body while keeping the knife parallel to the cutting board. Keep going until you have almost cut through, but keep the back part attached.

2 The innards are on top, so slice these off.

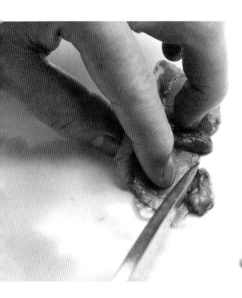

3 Cut off any parts that stick out to tidy up the shape.

4 Rinse in water, and make a cut using the heel of the knife.

The texture of the surf clam scallop

Two kinds of sushi are made from the surf clam: one is made from the body of the surf clam and is called *aoyagi*, and the other is made from the scallop or adductor muscle, and is called *kobashira*. Most of a shellfish's muscles are striated, but adductor muscles contain both striated and smooth muscles (see page 44). The translucent parts are straited muscles, and the opaque parts are smooth muscles. It's for this reason that scallops have a unique texture.

The science of cooking abalone

Black abalone is a sushi topping that's delicious raw or cooked. The distinctive texture of abalone is related to its collagen. Black abalone contains from 5 to 40 percent collagen in its muscles, from the center of its body outwards. The crunchy, chewy texture of raw abalone is caused by this collagen. When the collagen is cooked it goes through a transformation called gelatinization, and the meat becomes tender.

The cooking time for abalone is either short (between 15 to 30 minutes) or long (3 to 5 hours); this depends on what the chef prefers.

Black abalone turns tender if it is cooked at boiling point for about 30 minutes, which causes its collagen to break down. As the temperature of the abalone meat rises, enzymes get to work breaking down some of its protein, causing an increase in peptides and amino acids, which also increases its umami flavor.

When the abalone is cooked for longer, the collagen breaks down further and the meat becomes more and more tender. This further breaking down of the collagen leads to an increase in peptides in the meat, further enhancing the umami.

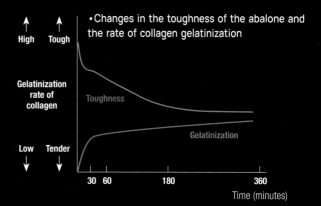

• Changes in the toughness of the abalone and the rate of collagen gelatinization

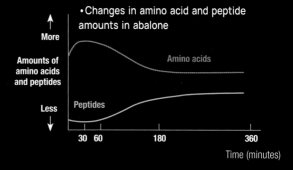

• Changes in amino acid and peptide amounts in abalone

The top graph above shows the change in toughness of abalone and gelatinization of the collagen. The toughness changes drastically at around 30 minutes of cooking, when the collagen breaks down rapidly and becomes gelatinized. The lower graph above shows the correlation between cooking time and changes in the amounts of amino acids and peptides in abalone. At 30 minutes of cooking the amino acids have increased, but the peptides have hardly increased. After 30 minutes of cooking, the collagen becomes more gelatinized and breaks down further, and the peptides start to increase. The amino acids have decreased because they have dissolved out into the cooking liquid.

Differences in umami when abalone is cooked for a short time vs. a long time

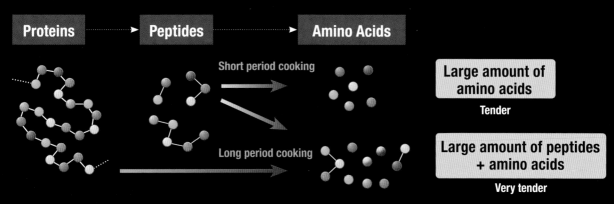

* The abalone becomes tender after about 30 minutes when the collagen is broken down.

Rinsing Surf Clam Scallops

When rinsing the scallops or adductor muscles of the surf clam, sometimes salt water is used rather than fresh water. This has about a 3 to 4 percent salt concentration, about the same as seawater. This salt water is called *tateshio* in Japanese.

Shellfish contain about 0.8 percent salt. The salt content of raw fish is about 0.2 percent, so washing with fresh water will not affect the taste. However, when shellfish are rinsed in fresh water, the water penetrates the surface of the shellfish, making it taste watery. Rinsing shellfish in salt water prevents this from happening.

Tateshio salt water is not only used to rinse shellfish, but to flavor fillets of fish. It does not dehydrate the fish and cause it to shrink, and the salty flavor penetrates the fish evenly.

The crystal structure of salt

The main component of salt is sodium chloride which has the chemical formula NaCl; it is made up by the bonding of natrium ions (Na+) with chloride ions (Cl–) which forms crystals. Highly concentrated sodium chloride has ions that bond at equal strength from all sides, causing it to form beautifully regular cubic crystals.

Sushi restaurants use a variety of types of salt to suit their tastes. You'll find more information on page 120.

Pure sodium chloride forms beautiful cubic crystals. (Photo credit: The Salt Industry Center of Japan)

Squid

A variety of squid and cuttlefish, including bigfin reef squid, golden cuttlefish, swordtip squid, flying squid and firefly squid, appear year round as sushi toppings. Until the 1930s, squid used as a sushi topping was always simmered or boiled, but in recent years raw squid is used too.

Squid
(*Ika*)

There are several types of squid and cuttlefish depending on the time of year, and eating sushi made with them is an enjoyable way to mark the seasons.

From spring to summer, bigfin reef squid, which is called the "king of squid," is in season. It's also called "water squid" because its body is transparent like water when it's swimming in the sea. It is thick and meaty with rich umami, and increases in flavor when it is matured.

From fall to winter, cuttlefish is in season, but the mature ones are preceded in August by new or baby cuttlefish, which are used whole, one per sushi. These whole baby cuttlefish have translucent bodies containing the umami that is unique to whole squid or cuttlefish, and are incredibly tender. However, cuttlefish goes off very quickly, and the season for the baby type is very short. Sushi aficionados look forward to this delicacy all year.

Squid and cuttlefish are worthy of notice for their nutritional value too. They are rich in an amino acid called taurine, which may help to reduce fatigue (see page 96).

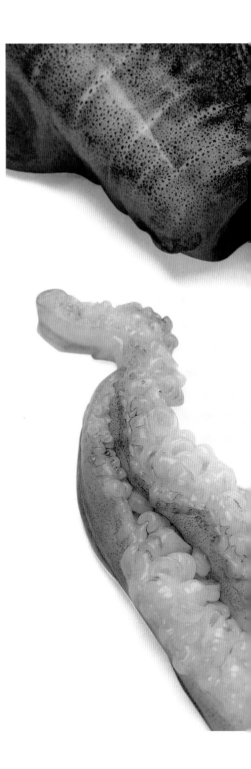

All About Squid and Cuttlefish

The skin of a squid or cuttlefish is made up of four layers, each of which consists of collagen. The fourth layer, the one right on the flesh, has collagen that clings to the body as if it has roots. To remove the skin, an effective method (although not used much at sushi restaurants) is to dunk the squid or cuttlefish for one or two seconds in boiling water. The skin will come off easily since collagen shrinks in heat. The appeal of squid or cuttlefish is its thick, rich meat and strong sweetness. Take care not to damage the meat as you remove the cuttlebone, and cut it up quickly. Be sure not to puncture the stomach when removing it.

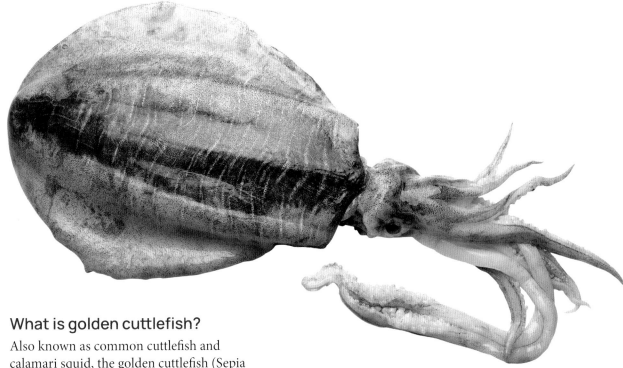

What is golden cuttlefish?

Also known as common cuttlefish and calamari squid, the golden cuttlefish (Sepia esculenta) is the most representative type of squid or cuttlefish at sushi restaurants. When it is small it is called "new cuttlefish" or "baby cuttlefish." In Japanese both squid and cuttlefish are called *ika*: golden cuttlefish is called *sumi-ika* while bigfin reef squid, which is also used a lot for sushi, is called *aori-ika*. In English the type with short bodies and tough bones is called cuttlefish, and the long type with soft bones is called squid, which includes bigfin reef squid and flying squid (*surume ika*).

The Sweetness of Squid and Cuttlefish

Although the flavor of squid and cuttlefish varies depending on the type, their distinctive sweetness comes from an abundance of sweet, umami-rich amino acids such as glycine and alanine. In addition, although the umami in fish is said to be inosinic acid, in squid and cuttlefish there are a lot of compounds related to the umami substance AMP (see page 49) that occurs naturally in their body. This accounts for the difference in flavors between fish and squid or cuttlefish.

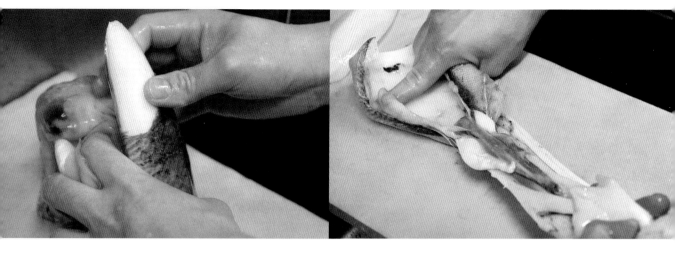

1 Make a slit in the center of the body from the tip of the head towards the eyes. Push out the cuttlebone.

2 Carefully peel off the outer skin and flesh surrounding the cuttlebone, and pull off the legs.

3 Grasping the end part, peel off the outer skin towards the bottom end. Grab onto the end of skin on the outer side of the body together with the fin, and peel it all off together with the thin inner skin. Take out the stomach, taking care not to puncture it, and remove the innards.

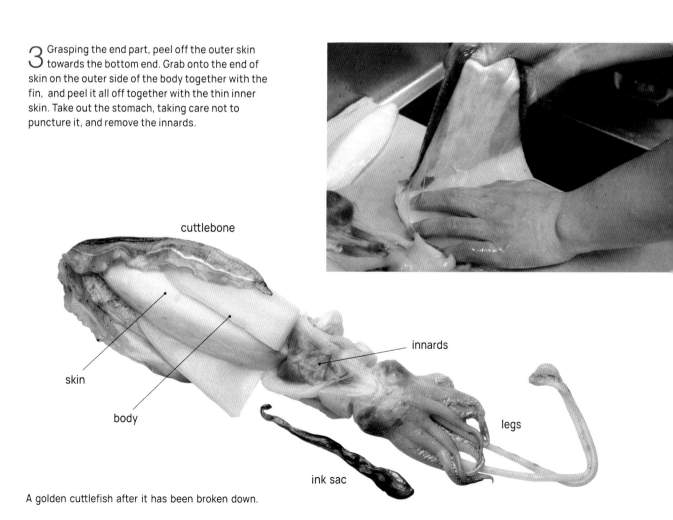

cuttlebone

skin

body

ink sac

innards

legs

A golden cuttlefish after it has been broken down.

Octopus

A large variety of octopuses — generally called *tako* — are eaten in Japan, but the ones seen most commonly as sushi toppings are the common octopus (Octopus sinensis; *madako* in Japanese), giant Pacific octopus (Enteroctopus dofleini; *mizudako*) and webfoot octopus (Amphioctopus fangsiao, *iidako*). The common octopus is in season from the fall to the winter, the giant Pacific octopus from fall to spring, and the webfoot octopus from winter to spring. Since the texture and flavor of octopus can vary depending on how it's massaged and cooked, each sushi restaurant shows off their own techniques when preparing it.

The most often-used type of octopus at sushi restaurants is the *madako* or common octopus. When fresh, it has a grayish-white color and spots on its body; the suckers have bounce and still have enough strength to stick to you. If this isn't the case, it means the octopus is not fresh. Another way to tell that an octopus isn't fresh is if the skin comes off easily when it's simmered.

Octopuses are rich in an amino acid called taurine, said to have various health benefits, such as improving the function of the liver and preventing the hardening of the arteries, as well as anti-inflammatory properties. For this reason, there's an old saying in Japan, "an octopus seller doesn't have lung disease."

If an octopus is not handled properly it can become too tough to chew. But if it is well massaged and beaten to break apart the structure of the muscles and soften up the muscle fibres before it's cooked, it will be tender and good to eat.

Cooking octopus

The most common kind of cooking method for octopus in Japan is called *sakura-ni* or "cherry blossom stewing," which means the octopus is cooked in soy sauce, sugar and sake. Some places cook octopus in hoji tea, sake or water.

At Sushi Takahashi, we cook octopus in a liquid made of 1 part mirin, 1 part soy sauce, 2–3 parts sugar, 3 parts sake and 3 parts water. This is combined and brought to a boil in a pan, and the octopus legs, which have been rinsed in water and massaged with salt, are put in. The heat is then turned off, the pan is covered with two sheets of aluminum foil, and the whole pan is put into a steamer and steamed for one hour. With this method the protein becomes tender, and the octopus has a nice looking finish with the skin left intact. When the octopus has been cooked, it's left as is at room temperature, and eaten on the same day.

The Muscles of Squid, Cuttlefish and Octopus

The fish and seafood used as sushi toppings can be largely divided into two types: vertebrates and invertebrates. The vertebrates are fish such as sea bream, sea bass and tuna, while the invertebrates include octopus, squid, cuttlefish and clams, as well as anthropods such as shrimp and crab. Vertebrates have their bone structures inside their bodies, and the bones are connected to each other to support the structure of those bodies. These bones are connected to muscles, and these muscles move the bones.

On the other hand, invertebrates have their bones outside their bodies (exoskeletons), and the muscles on the insides of the bones move their bodies. They have muscle structures that move freely.

These differences in muscle and skeletal structure are a key reason why the flavors and textures of squid, cuttlefish and octopus differ from those of fish.

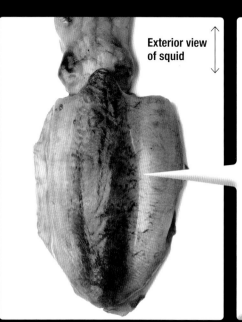

Exterior view of squid

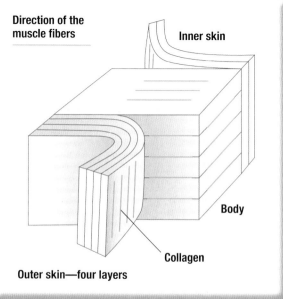

Direction of the muscle fibers

Inner skin

Body

Collagen

Outer skin—four layers

Squid and cuttlefish

- The muscle fibers of a squid or cuttlefish are perpendicular to its direction, in other words they circle the body in parallel to each other.
- The two outer layers of skin can be removed easily, but the two inner layers are stuck fast to the body and are hard to peel off.
- The outermost layer of skin and the two layers below it are pigmented, so if you remove these the meat will have a white color after it's cooked.
- Squid and cuttlefish have about 80 percent water content, which is about 10 percent more than other fish and seafood. This means a lot of moisture escapes when they are cooked, so they can become tough.

Stewing squid or cuttlefish

When the skin surrounding squid and cuttlefish is heated to around 131°F (55°C), it starts to shrink. To cook squid so that it is tender, it is either cooked for a short time until the internal temperature reaches 151°F (66°C), or cooked at a high temperature that exceeds 176°F (80°C) for more than 10 minutes, until the meat of the body breaks down and the collagen becomes gelatinized.

Octopus

- The muscle fibers of an octopus do not run in one direction. Muscles that extend in different directions are tangled together in a complex pattern.
- One method of tenderizing octopus is to freeze it when raw. This breaks down the cells and structure of the body.

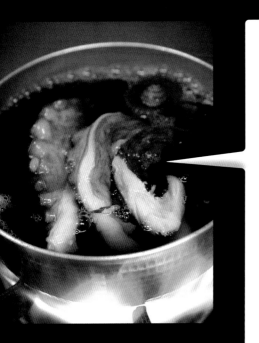

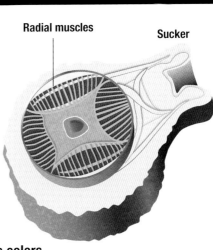

Radial muscles   Sucker

Octopus colors

The octopus has a pigment called ommochrome, which has red, yellow, brown and black colors. Ommochrome is contained in cells called chromatophores. Because these chromatophores shrink and stretch together with the muscles, the color of the octopus changes. This is why an octopus can quickly change its colors depending on its surroundings. The reason why octopus turns red when it's boiled is because the proteins in its muscles change due to heat, and the shape of the chromatophores changes.

Rubbing an octopus with salt removes its sliminess. The slimy substance on an octopus is mostly made up of glycoproteins called mucin, and since glycoproteins harden with salt, it becomes easier to remove the sliminess. As with squid and cuttlefish, the muscles of the octopus shrink drastically when they are cooked and can become tough. The muscles can be loosened up by vigorously massaging them beforehand, which helps avoid shrinkage when cooking. In addition, if the octopus is either cooked for a short time to a temperature where the collagen hasn't yet started to shrink, or for a long time at a high temperature until the collagen has gelatinized, it will be tender. The cooking times and methods vary depending on what type of result is desired.

Shrimp

え
び

Shrimp
(*Ebi*)

Shrimp have been used for sushi in Japan since the Edo period (1603–1868). Back then only boiled shrimp were used, but in recent times raw shrimp have become very popular too. Their bright color, sweetness, and delicious aroma makes an appealing and very popular sushi topping.

There are many types of shrimp in Japan, but the ones popular as sushi toppings include Japanese tiger shrimp (Marsupenaeus japonicus; *kuruma ebi* in Japanese), botan or spot shrimp (Pandalus nipponensis Yokoya; *botan ebi*) and sweet or shrimp (Pandalus eous; *amaebi*). Other shrimp used include white shrimp (Metapenaeopsis lata; *shiroebi*) and morotoge shrimp (Pandalopsis japonica Balss; *shimaebi*). Of all of these, tiger shrimp (kuruma ebi) is the star. It has a beautiful red and white color when it's cooked, and a sweet, deep umami flavor. It has this distinctive flavor because it contains a high amount of glycine, which is known for its strong sweetness amongst the various amino acids. However, if the shrimp is boiled for too long, this sweetness will just dissolve out into the water. If it is blanched quickly so that the inside remains raw, in a "medium rare" state, its essences will remain trapped inside, and it will retain a tender yet springy texture. The name of the tiger shrimp changes in Japanese depending on its size; small ones care called *saimaki ebi* or just *saimaki*, and large ones are called *kuruma ebi*.

Why Do Shrimp Turn Red When Boiled?

Some shrimp such as botan shrimp and sweet shrimp are a red color when they are raw, while others like tiger shrimp and morotoge shrimp are black. This difference in color is connected to the depth of the waters in their habitats. The shallower the water, the blacker the shrimp; ones that live in deep waters have red bodies.

This red is a pigment called astaxanthin. This is a natural pigment that belongs to the same group of natural yellow, red or orange pigments called carotenoids in carrots and tomatoes.

Black colored shrimp also contain astaxanthin. When the shrimp are raw, the astaxanthin is bound with protein, so the red color does not reveal itself and has a blackish purple color. But when the shrimp are cooked, the protein in them changes, revealing the inherent red color of the astaxanthin.

Shell color

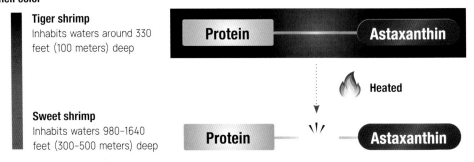

Tiger shrimp
Inhabits waters around 330 feet (100 meters) deep

Sweet shrimp
Inhabits waters 980–1640 feet (300–500 meters) deep

クルマエビ

Tiger Shrimp (*Kuruma ebi*)

As a rule, tiger shrimps are bought and sold live in Japan. They are used as sushi toppings raw or cooked. A lot of what is available is farmed, but ones caught in the wild are often seen too; these have very bright striped markings when they are cooked.

アマエビ

Sweet Shrimp (*Amaebi*)

The melting texture of sweet shrimp makes this a popular sushi topping. Although the amount of sweet-tasting glycine is less in these shrimp than in other varieties, they still taste sweet. This is because of the meltingly soft texture of their proteins. When the texture is this soft, the sweetness can be tasted more on the tongue. When these shrimp are cooked, the proteins toughen up, the texture becomes harder and they don't taste sweet anymore. Therefore sweet shrimp are best eaten raw.

ボタンエビ

Botan Shrimp (*Botan ebi*)

The word *botan* means peony in Japanese, and as the name indicates, these shrimp have a showy color like peony flowers. They also have a nice rich texture and refined sweetness. They are a high-class sushi topping, served raw.

蝦蛄

Mantis Shrimp
(*Shako*)

Mantis Shrimp

Mantis shrimp is one of the sushi toppings that typifies Edomae (traditional Tokyo-style) sushi. Although they can be eaten raw, in most cases they are boiled in salt water as soon as they are caught and brought to sushi restaurants in that state. These ready-boiled shrimp are then immersed in a flavorful simmering liquid — an age old process called *tsukekomi* — in order to marry well with sushi rice. Mantis shrimp have two seasons: the spring and the fall. Spring mantis shrimp in particular are packed with eggs called *katsubushi*, and are highly prized for that reason.

Although mantis shrimp look like shrimp and are even called shrimp, they are actually not shrimp. They are hard to peel unless they are very fresh, and because it requires skill to peel them properly, the ones that appear in sushi display cases at restaurants have been peeled and processed at the source. If fresh mantis shrimp are obtained, their hard shells are taken off with scissors. A favorite variety of mantis shrimp is called *koshiba*, caught at Koshiba in Kanagawa Prefecture. These koshiba mantis shrimp have a reputation for being delicious even when they've been boiled, and are very popular. Mantis shrimp are brushed with a concentrated sauce after they have been placed on the ball of sushi rice.

What is a mantis shrimp?

Mantis shrimp look rather grotesque. Although they have a light gray color when raw, they become purple when boiled. In some parts of Japan they are called *gasa ebi* rather than the usual *shako*.

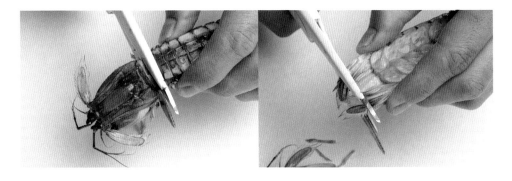

1 The head is cut off with scissors.

2 The mantis shrimp is flipped over and the tip of the tail is cut.

3 The left and right sides are cut off as shown.

4 The thin shell on the stomach side is removed.

5 The back shell is removed.

Conger Eel

穴子

Conger eel is an archetypal cooked sushi topping. Conger eel that has been processed quickly while still fresh and cooked to a tender plump state is not only soft when it's eaten right away, it remains that way even after some time has passed, which makes it ideal for take-out sushi.

Conger Eel
(*Anago*)

Conger eels versus freshwater eels

Although conger eels (Conger myriaster; *anago* in Japanese) and the eels known as *unagi* (Anguilla japonica) may seem similar, they belong to different categories biologically speaking. They also have different habitats, look different and of course taste different too. Conger eels are sea creatures who live out their lives in salt water, but *unagi* are freshwater eels that swim up rivers to lakes or ponds after spawning.

Fat-rich conger eel, with its dense flesh that has been simmered in a cooking liquid made of soy sauce and sugar, has a light, meltingly tender mouthfeel. This is particularly true of the conger eel caught in Tokyo Bay, called *edomae anago*, whose peak season is from mid July to early September.

Conger eel is swiftly broken down as soon as it's killed, before rigor mortis sets in, and cooked in plenty of liquid so that it practically dances in it (see page 108). To ensure the eel bought by a sushi restaurant is fresh, it is often killed in front of the buyer, at the market. Many chefs cook it as soon as they get it back to their establishments.

Conger eel can be eaten year round, and there is year-round demand for it from customers too. In peak season, conger eel has plenty of fat on it and will cook up plump and tender, but the amount of fat and the texture of the flesh can differ depending on the season and where the eel was caught.

At Sushi Takahashi, the early-spring conger eel which has little fat on it, is reheated just before it's made into sushi, so that it's very soft. The oil-rich conger eel available from fall to winter is quickly broiled just before it's turned into sushi to add a nutty flavor. The cooking liquid is reduced to make the sauce that is brushed onto the eel. You could say that conger eel is a sushi topping that requires your full care and attention from the time it's killed, through its cooking process and until the sauce is made.

Filleting a conger eel

1 Place the eel with its back facing you*, and pierce through, between the eyes and the gills. Insert the knife somewhat diagonally from the side of the eel towards the head. Turn the blade of the knife toward the tail end.

* This method of opening up an eel from the back side is used in the Tokyo region. In the Osaka region, it's usually opened up from the belly side.

2 Cut along the center bone. Be careful with the angle of the blade, or you may cut through the bone.

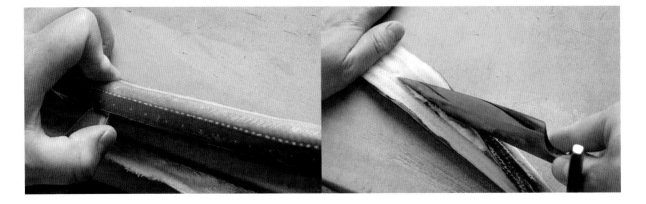

3 When you have cut about halfway through the eel, put your thumb against the back of the blade and pull as you keep cutting. When the blade reaches the anal area, cut through in one go.

4 When you have cut through to the tail, put the tip of the knife back in the head side and gently open up the eel. Make a cut along the center bone. Wiggle the blade along and fillet the eel completely.

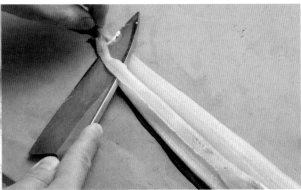

5 Cut the innards from the flesh, and pull off with your hands. Cut the center bone just where it's connected to the head.

6 Lay the blade flat under the center bone, and cut off the bone only.

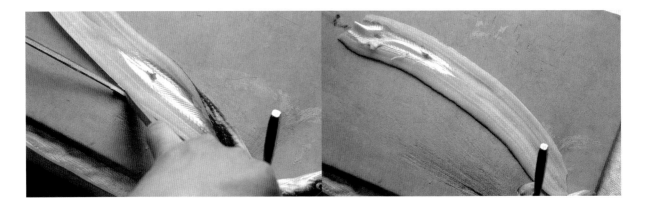

7 Take off the back fin.

8 Scrape off the dark red flesh (the *chiai*) and any sliminess on the surface, and cut off the head. Scrub the flesh as you rinse it in water. Drain off with the skin side facing up.

How to boil conger eel

Put 4¾ gallons (18 liters) of water in a pot, add ¾ cup (180 ml) mirin, ¾ cup (180 ml) soy sauce, 2½ cups (500 g) sugar and the conger eel. Put the pot on the heat, and when it has come to a boil skim off the scum. Place a small lid (a drop lid or *otoshibuta*) or a piece of crumpled up aluminum foil inside the pan, directly on top of the liquid, and simmer over low heat for 25 to 30 minutes. Leave the eel to cool in the pan, then take out and drain on a flat sieve or in a colander.

An eel's color changes according to the environment it inhabits

The color of eels

Most conger eels inhabit waters near coastlines that are less than 330 feet (100 meters) deep. During the day they hide in the shadows of rocks or bury themselves in sand. At nighttime they start their activity, and swim around looking for things to feed on. Although the freshwater eel (*unagi*) is covered with scales that are hard to see, the seawater conger eel has no scales at all and is covered with a slimy substance. Eels have dark colors which do not stand out, a trait they share with other creatures that live in shallow water. Those dark colors can differ, depending on the environment the creature inhabits, but the type of conger eel used for sushi has various dark colors with lines of white spots, called lateral lines. Lateral lines are the holes fish use to sense changes in water pressure and currents. These holes are large on a conger eel, and look like white spots.

Simmering Seafood

In sushi restaurant parlance, "simmering work" (*ni-shigoto*) means, as it says, to cook items by simmering them in liquid. Although this liquid used to always be a salty-sweet mixture, in recent years some places use a "salt simmering" method instead. The typical items cooked in liquid in this manner besides conger eel are octopus, mantis shrimp, Asian hard clams and abalone. Squid and scallops also used to be simmered, but these days they are more often made into raw sushi toppings instead.

The typical simmering liquid contains mirin, soy sauce and sugar. The amounts used and the length of time things are simmered for differ by the establishment — each sushi restaurant has its own flavors.

Simmering eels

The sliminess on the surface of the conger eels is removed before it is simmered. If water or salt are used for this task the flesh will become tough, so put the eels in a bowl and rub well until the slimy substance becomes bubbly, then rinse it off quickly.

Conger eels are cooked in two ways: quickly over high heat, a method called *sawani* in Japanese; or slowly for 15 to 20 minutes or more over low heat, and then left immersed in the cooking liquid—this method is called *tsukekomi*.

The quick sawani method is often used for small 6 to 8 inch (15 to 20 cm) eels called *meso anago*. The sliminess is removed with water, and the cooking liquid is brought to a boil before the eels are put in, turning to cook them through. The eels are then taken out and cooled on a sieve. They come out with a pale white color.

The slower tsukekomi method is used for large eels about 16 to 20 inches (40 to 50 cm) long. After the cooking liquid comes to a boil, the eels are simmered for 25 to 30 minutes, then left to cool in the cooking liquid so the flavors penetrate.

Simmering Asian hard clams

Put 2 parts Japanese sake, 1 part mirin, 3 parts water, 1.5 parts sugar and 1 part soy sauce in a pan, along with the clams. Heat the pan and maintain a temperature of 140°F (60°C) so the clams don't get tough as they cook.

Seasonings and the Tenderness of Eel

Fish and seafood are all collections of cells, so seasonings penetrate them after those cells are broken down by heat. When the cells are raw, their membranes protect them and seasonings cannot penetrate.

Conger eel is soft and tender when cooked because cooking takes place at a lower temperature than the temperature at which its collagen shrinks. Collagen shrinkage in meat occurs at 149°F (65°C), but at a lower temperature in fish. At Sushi Takahashi, we put the eels in boiling liquid for a short time to cook the surface, and then take them out to cool on a sieve. The surface of the just-cooked eels is around 212°F (100°C), but as they cool the heat is transferred from the surface to the interior. As the internal temperature does not exceed the collagen shrinkage temperature, the eels turn out tender.

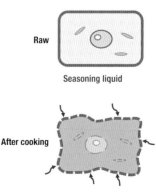

Raw

Seasoning liquid

After cooking

雲丹

Sea Urchin
(*Uni*)

Sea Urchin

Golden sea urchin on top of black nori-seaweed-wrapped rice is one of the most popular types of sushi. A good quality sea urchin has an unctuous texture, sweet flavor and the rich aroma of the sea.

Sea urchin is a fairly new sushi topping, and its peak season is from April to August. Sea urchin inhabits most coastal areas of Japan, and there are many varieties. The main ones used as sushi toppings include purple sea urchin (*murasaki uni*), bafun sea urchin (*bafun uni*), ezo purple sea urchin (*ezo murasaki uni*) and pink or red sea urchin (*aka uni*). Sea urchin is brought in from the source in shallow wooden boxes, and used as is. At the wholesale market the bafun sea urchin is called "red" because of its color when it's shelled, and ezo purple sea urchin is called "white."

What is a sea urchin?

The parts sold on the market are the reproductive organs—the testes and ovaries—of the sea urchin, which are inside the shell in five globules. Since sea urchin eat kombu and other types of seaweed depending on the area they inhabit, their taste, aroma and color varies according to their habitat and what they take in as food.

purple sea urchin

bafun sea urchin

The sea urchin at the bottom of the photo are bafun sea urchin, so called because they look like horse manure (*bafun*). The ones at the top with the sharp black spikes are purple sea urchin.

(Photo credit: Photo Work Freak Ltd. / Image Navi)

Purple sea urchin

Alum and sea urchin

Fresh sea urchin is firm and has a nice aroma, but when it is less fresh it falls apart easily and becomes watery. In order to prevent this. a lot of sea urchin is treated with the chemical compound alum, which hardens up protein. The cells in a sea urchin are made of protein, so if sea urchin is treated with alum these cells tighten up and the shape does not become soft. Fresh sea urchin is called *nama uni* (raw sea urchin) or *ita uni* (board sea urchin). In recent years *shio uni* (salt sea urchin), in sterilized or artificial sea water, is widely available too, but does not last as long as sea urchin treated with alum. The sea water soon becomes cloudy, so the sea urchin in it should be used as quickly as possible.

Color differences in sea urchin varieties

The color differs depending on the season, region, and between individual sea urchin.

Bafun
sea urchin

Purple
sea urchin

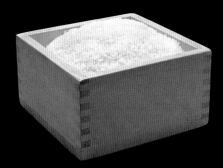

CHAPTER 2

THE SCIENCE OF SUSHI (PART 2):
RICE, VINEGAR AND OTHER INGREDIENTS

Rice

Many sushi chefs agree that sushi is "60 percent about the *shari* (sushi rice), and 40 percent about the *neta* (topping)." This means that even if you use the very best toppings, if the rice is no good the sushi won't be tasty. The ideal is sushi rice that doesn't fall apart when picked up, but dissolves gracefully when put into your mouth.

This hardly needs to be said, but sushi consists of fish or seafood on top of sushi rice, so the taste and texture of the rice have a big impact on how good the sushi is. The right kind of rice to suit the toppings has to be chosen, and then cooked and flavored with vinegar and salt, and in some cases sugar too.

However, if the sushi rice is too strongly flavored you won't be able to taste the fish on top of it. The sushi rice and the sushi topping have to form one unit, so that you can't serve the rice on its own or the topping on its own—they come together to form "sushi": that is the goal.

The texture of the sushi rice is as important as its flavor of course. It should not be too hard or too soft, and it should be cooked so that it melds perfectly with the topping when it's bitten into. In order to achieve this, it's important to know the state of the rice when it's cooked, and how it absorbs the sushi vinegar. In the past, there were *shari-ya*—chefs who specialized in cooking sushi rice. Making delicious sushi rice reliably is that difficult a task, and the fact that there used to be specialists who did this shows how important rice is to sushi.

All About Rice

 ## Types of rice

There are two types of Japanese rice: medium grain rice (*uruchi*), and glutinous short grain sticky rice (*mochi*). The type of rice eaten every day in Japan is uruchi rice. Of the around 900* varieties of rice registered in Japan, around 290 are grown for everyday consumption.

In terms of area used to grow that rice, 33 percent of the total area is devoted to the variety called Koshihikari, followed by Hitomebore, Hinohikari, Akitakomachi, Nanatsuboshi, Haenuki, Kinuhikari, Masshigura, Asahinoyume and Yumepirika, in that order. Since there are around 290 different varieties of uruchi rice, sushi chefs search for the rice they want to use, and on occasion will blend several varieties together. The varieties most used for sushi rice are Koshihikari, Hitomebore, Akitakomachi, Silky Pearl and Milky Queen. Each has different proportions of amylopectin and amylose (see page 116) as well as different amounts of proteins, so each has its own unique stickiness and texture.

Koshihikari, Hitomebore and Akitakomachi contain around 17 to 18 percent amylose, but Milky Queen and Silky Pearl only contain 4 to 11 percent, so they are called low-amylose rices. Low-amylose rice types have a high amount of amylopectin, which means they have a stronger stickiness.

Koshihikari also has its supporters because it tastes good when it's cool.

Ideal Rice for Sushi Rice

- The grains are small and uniform
- The grains are white, translucent and have luster
- The grains have a weight to them
- The grains are dried properly

Amylose percentage (%) = the amount of amylose in the rice's starch

 ## New harvest rice and old rice

There are two criteria that define "new harvest rice." One is that it applies to rice harvested between November 1st and October 31st of the following year. The other is that it applies to rice that is polished and packed in the year it's harvested up until December 31st of that year (this is the Japan Food Labeling Standard). Any rice older than that is considered "old rice."

One often hears the opinion "old rice is better suited to sushi than new harvest rice." The reasoning behind this is that while old rice has a smooth texture when cooked, new harvest rice is sticky, making it difficult to achieve the correct texture for sushi rice. The "old rice" in this case doesn't mean very old rice, but rather rice that has been harvested in the preceding year. There are sushi restaurants who only use old rice, and others that blend old and new rice. Each chef figures out their best cooking methods and how to blend it with the sushi vinegar to come up with the ideal sushi rice.

Old rice is tougher than new harvest rice, and is said to be 2–3 percent less absorbent.

Rice Grain Stable Supply Securing Support Organization, "Report on Rice-growing Trends by Variety in 2018."

Amylose and amylopectin

Polished white rice is composed of about 78 percent carbohydrate (in other words combined sugars and fiber), most of which is starch. Starch consists of chains of glucose beads. When these glucose beads are connected in a straight line, the starch is amylose, but if the beads branch out occasionally the starch is amylopectin. When branches of amylopectin get tangled up in water, this produces a strong sticky texture.

The amount of amylose in starch is called the amylose percentage. The stickiness of rice largely depends on this amylose percentage. The two main Asian rices are Indica and Japonica. Long grain Indica rice contains 17 to 27 percent amylose and less amylopectin, so the grains have hardly any stickiness and are separate. Japonica rice on the other hand contains 16 to 18 percent amylose, so it has a fair amount of stickiness. Rice which contains 0 percent amylose, with starch made up solely of amylopectin is glutinous rice (*mochi*), which has a very strong stickiness.

In recent years, there are many rice varieties with a very low amount of amylose, around 4 to 11 percent, called low-amylose rice.

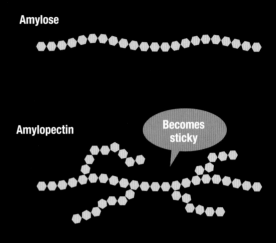

Amylose

Amylopectin

Becomes sticky

 ## Starch gelatinization

The main change that occurs with starch is gelatinization. When starch that does not dissolve in cold or room-temperature water is heated, it becomes translucent and sticky just like glue or thick gelatin. This is gelatinization. The name for starch before it becomes gelatinized is β (beta) starch, and the name for starch after gelatinization is α (alpha) starch.

The starch in rice is made up of amylose, which are straight strands of glucose, and amylopectin, which are branched-out strands of glucose. The structure of the starch is so dense that not even water molecules can get in. However, when heated to around 140 to 149°F (60 to 65°C), this structure loosens up, and water molecules can get in between the strands. This is how rice becomes sticky.

If gelatinized starch is allowed to cool down, the stickiness gradually lessens. This is called the aging of starch.

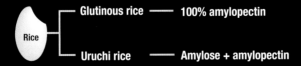

Rice —┬— Glutinous rice —— 100% amylopectin
      └— Uruchi rice —— Amylose + amylopectin

Sushi rice and vinegar

The vinegar mixture used to season sushi rice, *awase-zu*, is mixed in to freshly cooked hot rice so that the vinegar penetrates the grains well. Since freshly cooked rice is very hot (according to measurements made by the editorial staff, the freshly cooked rice at Sushi Takahashi is 208°F [98°C]) and some of the water contained inside the grains is steam, the volume of each freshly cooked grain increases. As the rice cools, the steam inside the grains turns back into water, and the grains shrink down. This is the point when the vinegar seasoning is absorbed into the grains. And since the hotter the rice, the faster the vinegar is absorbed, when the vinegar is mixed with freshly cooked rice it penetrates it very rapidly.

According to a study that compared the absorption rates of sushi vinegar mixed into rice that was at 176°F (80°C), 122°F (50°C) and 68°F (20°C), the sushi vinegar was absorbed better by the hotter rice.

Variations In how rice cooks

When rice is cooked, the rice on the top, middle and bottom of the cooker has differently shaped grains and textures. When we cook rice at Sushi Takahashi (see page 122), the rice on the top is on the dry side, and the rice on the bottom has been crushed by the weight of the rice above it and is flat. In addition the rice on the bottom of the pot is burned because the heat is raised high at the end of the cooking process. The only grains that have the proper shape and plump texture are the ones in the middle. For this reason, at Sushi Takahashi, not only do we remove the burned rice at the bottom, we also remove the flattened grains in that area and the dry ones at the top. If there are variations in the size and shape as well as the surface stickiness of the grains, not only does it affect the appearance of the sushi, but it affects the taste.

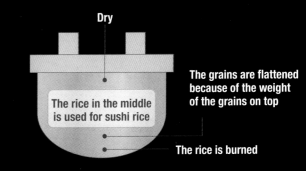

Dry

The grains are flattened because of the weight of the grains on top

The rice in the middle is used for sushi rice

The rice is burned

Vinegar (*Su*)

Types of Vinegar

Sushi is said to have originated as *narezushi*, a dish where fish is fermented with salt and rice and has a distinctive sourness. The sourness in modern sushi is provided by vinegar, an indispensable ingredient.

Nowadays, when we think of sushi, we are likely to think first and foremost of what is known as *nigirizushi*—a topping on a ball of rice, which is a long way from sushi's narezushi origins as a fermented product of fish, salt and rice. After narezushi, *oshizushi* (pressed sushi) eventually appeared in the Osaka region, but in the nineteenth century, to suit the impatient nature of the citizens of Edo (modern Tokyo), a type of sushi that didn't need to be fermented was born. The sour flavor was achieved with vinegar, and was eaten one piece at a time.

The type of vinegar used for this new kind of sushi was *kasu-zu*, made with sake lees. This vinegar has a red color, so it's also called red vinegar. These days most sushi restaurants use rice vinegar: it does not have a strong color so does not affect the color of the rice, allowing contrast with the toppings; and it doesn't have an overassertive flavor. However, lately, there are an increasing number of restaurants that utilize red vinegar for their sushi, for its aroma and well-rounded flavor.

Black vinegar

Making sushi vinegar

Put vinegar (10 parts rice vinegar: 1 part red vinegar: 1 part black vinegar) in a pan. Add sugar, salt and water, bring to a boil and leave to cool.

The vinegars in use at Sushi Takahashi

Red vinegar

Rice vinegar

The Colors of Black and Red Vinegar

Both black and red vinegar have color, because the base ingredients for each are fermented and aged for a long time. During this process, a chemical reaction called the Maillard reaction takes place. This is a reaction between sugars and proteins, which causes the vinegar to take on a dark brown or red color. Because black and red vinegars have a longer fermenting and aging time compared to most other edible vinegars, they contain large amounts of amino acids and sugars and are dark in color. The color varies depending on the base ingredients used, and as the photo here shows, even black vinegar can have a red hue, and red vinegar can have a black color.

Salt (*Shio*)

All About Salt

As discussed in the vinegar section on the previous page, sushi was originally a fermented product made with fish, salt and rice. Salt is indispensable to sushi. Not only does it add flavor, it firms up the fish and keeps it fresh for longer. Let's take a closer look at some of the properties of salt.

There are many types of salt, with different manufacturing methods. Sushi chefs choose the salt best suited to them from the hundreds of types available. Are the grains separate or not? Does the salt dissolve easily or not? How much magnesium and other minerals does it contain? The characteristics of these many different types of salt largely depend on how they are manufactured. Even if they start out as sea salt or rock salt, when the salt is dissolved and reduced, it loses its original character and just becomes salt.

Sea water with a high amount of salt is called *kansui*, and the salt made by cooking it down is called *sengo* salt. Natural sea salt is often said to have a mild, well-rounded flavor. This is most likely because it often contains minerals other than sodium chloride. Pots called *tategama* and *hiragama* are used to cook down the salt; tategama have a vacuum tank–like shape, and hiragama are square or round.

Salt made in tategama has even, cubic crystals; it dissolves easily, gets sticky easily and feels heavy. Even when salt is cooked down in hiragama, the results can vary depending on the method used; when it's cooked over high heat, a strong convection current occurs within the vessel, making the crystals more even in shape. However the salt cooked is still uneven, so it has a structure that looks like many small crystals stuck together. On the other hand, when the salt is reduced slowly so that a convection current is not formed, the crystals are crunchy and flaky.

The crystal structures of salt

Salt has various crystal structures. Although salt is white, each crystal is colorless and transparent. When a lot of crystals are gathered together, light reflects off the bumpy surfaces unevenly, which is why salt looks white.

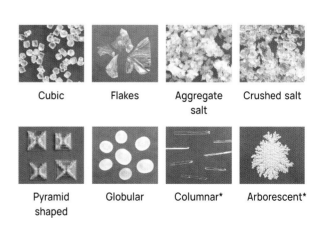

| Cubic | Flakes | Aggregate salt | Crushed salt |

| Pyramid shaped | Globular | Columnar* | Arborescent* |

*These crystal formations only result from very special manufacturing methods, and are hardly ever used for edible salt.

(Research and image source: The Salt Industry Center of Japan)

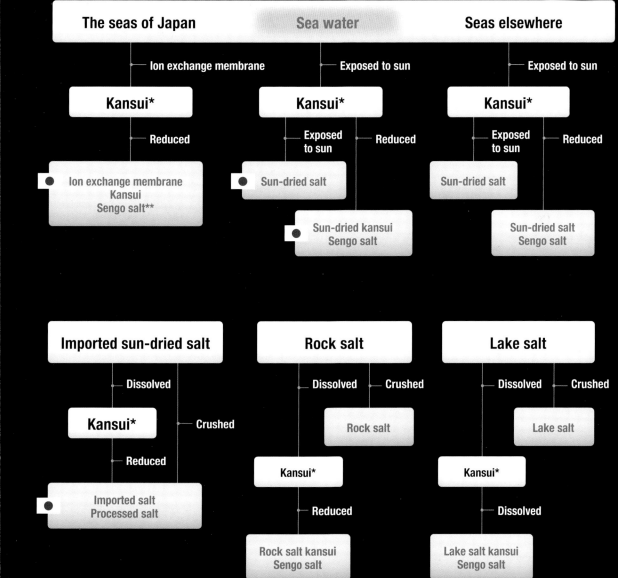

The seas of Japan — Ion exchange membrane → **Kansui*** — Reduced → ● Ion exchange membrane Kansui Sengo salt**

Sea water — Exposed to sun → **Kansui*** — Exposed to sun → ● Sun-dried salt | Reduced → ● Sun-dried kansui Sengo salt

Seas elsewhere — Exposed to sun → **Kansui*** — Exposed to sun → Sun-dried salt | Reduced → Sun-dried salt Sengo salt

Imported sun-dried salt — Dissolved → **Kansui*** — Reduced → ● Imported salt Processed salt | Crushed →

Rock salt — Dissolved → **Kansui*** — Reduced → Rock salt kansui Sengo salt | Crushed → Rock salt

Lake salt — Dissolved → **Kansui*** — Dissolved → Lake salt kansui Sengo salt | Crushed → Lake salt

● [*Japanese flag*] = Japanese domestic product
* Kansui = sea water with a high amount of salt
** Sengo salt = kansui reduced to produce salt

The salt names are based on documents from The Salt Industry Center of Japan and organized by manufacturing method.

Cooking Rice

To cook rice is to make the rice absorb water, and to gelatinize its starch with heat and water (see page 116). Even if the rice grains and water are separate to start in the pot, the water is totally absorbed by the rice, which then reaches the right degree of stickiness and texture. Rice that is cooked properly better absorbs the sushi vinegar, and becomes sushi rice that marries well with the toppings.

The quality of the sushi rice is inseparable from the quality of the sushi as a whole, and each chef has their own way of cooking the rice. Rather than an electric or gas-powered rice cooker, many restaurants use an old fashioned *hagama* pot to cook their rice. Sushi Takahashi is one such place. A heavy cast-iron hagama pot with a thick lid is used, and a large amount of water is put in. The lid is held down with a weight to allow almost no steam to escape and to pressurize the pot. Since the rice is cooked over high heat with little water relative to the amount of rice, the bottom does get burned. But it's because the heat is high enough to produce this burned part that the rice is soft and tender, yet has the right amount of firmness. At Sushi Takahashi many subtle adjustments have been made to this cooking process over the years, to arrive at our perfect method.

The method of cooking rice at Sushi Takahashi

First the rice is put in a bowl, water is added, and the rice is rinsed rapidly while stirring it quickly. The water is discarded and the rice put back in the bowl and stirred around to polish the grains. This process is repeated three times. If the rice is rinsed any more than this, the starch and protein will get washed out and the grains will shrink. The rice is returned to the bowl and soaked in water for 30 minutes, drained into a sieve, left to drain off for a minute, then put into the hagama pot. If the rice is left for too long in the sieve the grain will dry out and break up easily.

Rice to water ratio

Rice	Water
10 rice cooker cups	5 cups (1200 ml)

Rice to Water Ratio

Turn the heat to high

⋯⋯⋯⋯ 15 minutes (after bringing to a boil)

↓

Medium heat

⋯⋯⋯⋯ 15 minutes

↓

High heat

⋯⋯⋯⋯ 1 minute (evaporate remaining water here)

↓

Turn off the heat

⋯⋯⋯⋯ 20 minutes (let it rest and steam)

↓

Transfer the rice to wooden container

A large round wooden container called a *sharihan* is wiped with a wrung-out kitchen cloth. The freshly cooked rice is tipped out into the container. By just turning the hagama pot upside down over the container, the rice comes out cleanly. Because the rice is cooked with a relatively small amount of water, the bottom is a little burned. The burned part is removed cleanly with a rice paddle. Only the rice in the middle part is used. Although this method results in rice that's on the firm side, it is the perfect consistency for sushi rice.

Preparing Sushi Rice

When freshly cooked rice is combined with sushi vinegar, it becomes sushi rice for the first time. The sushi vinegar is sprinkled evenly onto the rice in the wooden container, and the rice is stirred up with a rice paddle using a cutting motion. When the sushi vinegar has permeated the rice and there are no lumps left, the rice is pushed to one side of the container. It's then transferred to another container called an *ohitsu* before it's turned into sushi.

1 The sushi vinegar is made in advance. Swirl the vinegar over the center of the top part of the rice, where the burned part (see page 123) has been removed.

2 Break down the mound of rice, and stir up the rice from the bottom.

3 When the sushi vinegar has permeated the rice evenly, spread the rice out in the container.

5 Wrap the rice in a kitchen towel, taking care not to crush the grains. Push the rice to one side of the container.

6 Transfer the rice to a container with a "keep warm" function to keep it warm until it's time to make it into sushi.

4 Keep fanning the rice as you stir it so that it will have a shiny finish.

Temperature Changes in Sushi Rice

These are the changes in temperature of the rice at the time it's freshly cooked, transferred to the wooden container, then transferred to the keep-warm container. Rice that is 208°F (98°C) when freshly cooked goes down to 138°F (59°C) by the time the burned part has been removed and the sushi vinegar has been poured over it. After finishing stirring with the rice paddle, the temperature is 109°F (43°C).

The preset temperature inside the keep-warm container (such as an electric rice cooker) is around 158°F (70°C). When the rice is transferred to the keep-warm container, its temperature rises a little, to 115°F (46°C). The temperature stays at around 109°F (43°C) until the rice is transferred again to a wooden *ohitsu* container just before it's made into sushi. When rice is made into sushi at that temperature, it's a little bit cooler by the time it reaches the customer—that temperature is called "the temperature of the skin," or body temperature.

Changes in rice temperature

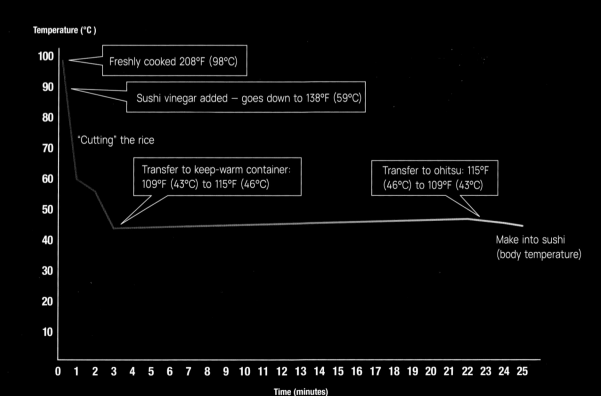

Temperature (°C)

Freshly cooked 208°F (98°C)

Sushi vinegar added – goes down to 138°F (59°C)

"Cutting" the rice

Transfer to keep-warm container: 109°F (43°C) to 115°F (46°C)

Transfer to ohitsu: 115°F (46°C) to 109°F (43°C)

Make into sushi (body temperature)

Time (minutes)

* Measured by the editorial staff

Nikiri Sauce for Fish

Nikiri is a light sauce brushed onto sushi just before it's served to the customer. It has a soy-sauce base to which mirin, dashi stock and so on are added in a variety of ways.

Although there is a method of eating sushi by dipping it into plain soy sauce in a small dish, many sushi chefs that serve Edomae (traditional Tokyo-style) sushi brush a soy-sauce-based sauce directly onto the sushi just before serving. This sauce is called nikiri, made by combining soy sauce, sake, and mirin—or soy sauce, sake and dashi stock—there are many styles. In all cases the alcohol in the sake and mirin is cooked off in a process called *nikiru*, which is where the name for the sauce comes from. The nikiri sauce at Sushi Takahashi uses equal amounts of soy sauce and mirin, cooked in a pan to evaporate the alcohol. The amount of nikiri brushed onto the topping is carefully calculated so that it doesn't overwhelm the fish.

煮切り

Nikiri
A specially prepared soy-sauce mixture that is brushed onto sushi before serving

Nitsume Sauce for Eel

Nitsume is a rich, heavy, concentrated sauce. At sushi restaurants the name is shortened to *tsume*. It is usually made by adding sugar and/or mirin to the liquid that conger eel has been cooked in. It is then cooked down to reduce and concentrate it.

The simmering liquid for conger eel (*anago*), an indispensable Edomae (traditional Tokyo-style) sushi topping, is used to make nikiri sauce (see opposite); the heads and bones that were removed before cooking are used to make a dashi stock that is added to the liquid, with soy sauce, sugar and sake; or soy sauce and mirin. This is cooked down to a thick, viscous sauce called nitsume. Some sushi restaurants make a fresh batch when the previous batch is finished; others keep adding to the previous nitsume, and make their "secret sauce" a feature. Besides conger eel, nitsume is brushed onto sushi toppings that have been simmered in a flavorful liquid, like mantis shrimp and Asian hard clam.

煮詰め

Nitsume
A condensed sauce made from conger eel broth

Sugar and Mirin: The Sweet Ingredients

The sweet ingredients used for sushi are sugar and mirin, a sweet, fortified rice liquor. Not only do these two ingredients add sweetness, they take the edge off any sourness or bitterness, add shine, and preserve the food for longer.

Sugar and Mirin

Sugar and mirin are mostly used in the simmering liquid for cooked sushi toppings, as well as in the vinegar that is used to season sushi rice. Either sugar, mirin or both are used in the simmering liquid; however, many sushi restaurants do not use sugar to make their sushi vinegar, as this is not a traditional practice.

But from the 1950s onwards, when sugar became widely available in Japan, a lot of sushi restaurants started adding sugar to their sushi vinegar. The main reasons for this were that sugar made the rice shinier, and also retarded the degradation of the starches in the rice, helping it keep longer.

The sweet qualities of sugar and mirin differ. This is because they contain different types of sugars. The sweetness of sugar made from sugar cane or sugar beets comes mainly from sucrose. The sweetness of mirin comes from the long process of breaking down and converting the starches in the rice from which mirin is made into glucose, maltose and oligosaccharide. Mirin has a very warm sweetness for this reason.

The reason why foods become shiny when mirin is added is because it contains glucose, the shiniest of all the sugars. When mirin is used in cooking, the alcohol it contains helps to prevent fish and seafood from breaking apart. In addition, because of its rich aroma it can reduce fishy odors too.

The Difference Between Hon Mirin and Mirin Seasoning

Hon mirin

Hon mirin or "real mirin" is made by combining glutinous rice and rice koji (*uruchi* rice inoculated with the *Aspergillus oryzae* mold) with shochu liquor. It is then saccharified and matured. It contains 45 percent sugar and about 14 percent alcohol, and is classified as an alcoholic beverage by Japanese liquor laws. It will keep for more than a year after it's opened.

Mirin seasoning

The ingredients for mirin seasoning are sugars such as glucose or malt syrup, seasonings and acids. It contains around 60 percent sugar and less than 1 percent salt. Since it also contains less than 1 percent alcohol it is not classified as an alcohol by Japanese liquor laws, and is sold at a lower price than hon mirin. It should be refrigerated after opening and used up within two to three months.

The Effects of Mirin

• Adds smooth sweetness and shine

Compared to sugar, whose sweetness is almost all sucrose (a disaccharide), 80 to 90 percent of the sweetness of mirin is glucose (a monosaccharide). Since glucose has smaller molecules than sucrose, it penetrates food more easily, and imparts a softer sweetness than sugar does. In addition, when heated, mirin imparts a nutty aroma and shininess to food.

• Deep flavor, umami and aroma

Since mirin is made from glutinous rice using a complex process (see page 131), it contains an abundance of amino acids, peptides, organic acids and fragrant elements. Amino acids and peptides are sources of umami, and the acidity of the organic acids enhance the flavor of food. By combining all of these elements, mirin adds a deep flavor, umami and pleasant aroma to the foods it is added to.

• Penetrates and firms up food, reduces odors

Hon mirin contains alcohol. When alcohol is present, it speeds up the rate at which the flavors of other seasonings penetrate food, so the food becomes flavored more quickly. The alcohol also firms up vegetable cell structures, so it helps to prevent vegetables from falling apart. In addition, since alcohol evaporates at around 172°F (78°C), when mirin is cooked with fish the alcohol takes any fishy odors with it as it evaporates.

• Preserves and sterilizes

Mirin can help preserve and sterilize sushi. Mirin's combination of alcohol and organic acids, used in combination with other sushi seasonings, acids and salt, give it preserving and sterilizing qualities.

Various Types of Sugar

The types of sugar used most frequently in sushi restaurants are a superfine sugar called *johakuto*, a refined light brown sugar called *wasanbon*, a light brown sugar called *san on to*, and raw cane sugar called *kibizato*. The color and size of the crystals differ depending on the manufacturing method.

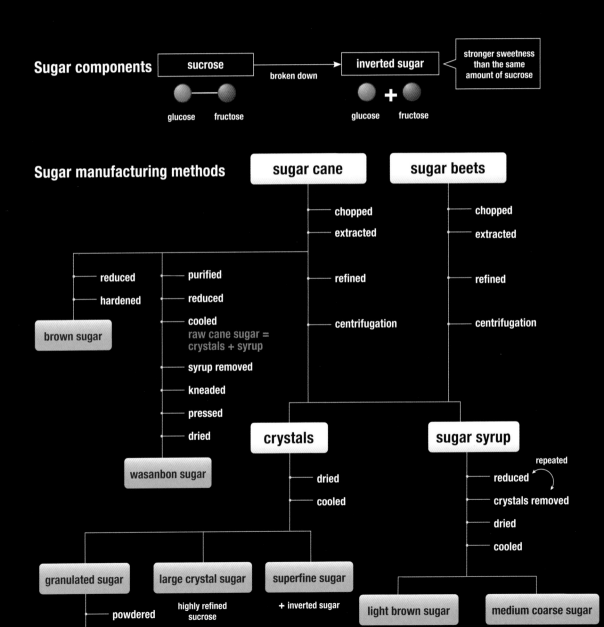

Sugar components

| sucrose | | inverted sugar | stronger sweetness than the same amount of sucrose |

broken down

glucose   fructose

glucose   +   fructose

Sugar manufacturing methods

sugar cane
sugar beets

- chopped
- extracted
- refined
- centrifugation

- chopped
- extracted
- refined
- centrifugation

- reduced
- hardened

brown sugar

- purified
- reduced
- cooled

raw cane sugar = crystals + syrup

- syrup removed
- kneaded
- pressed
- dried

wasanbon sugar

crystals

- dried
- cooled

sugar syrup

repeated

- reduced
- crystals removed
- dried
- cooled

granulated sugar   **large crystal sugar**   **superfine sugar**

- powdered

highly refined sucrose

+ inverted sugar

light brown sugar   **medium coarse sugar**

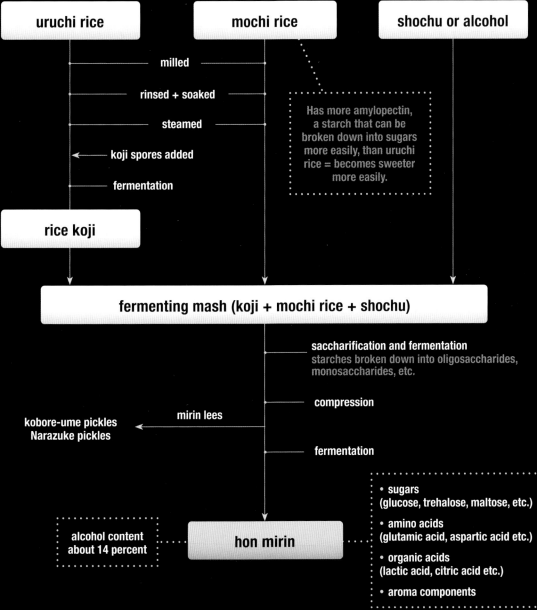

All About Wasabi

わ
さ
び

With its distinctive, sharp spiciness and refreshing aroma, wasabi is indispensable to nigirizushi. When a sushi chef starts grating fresh wasabi at the counter, that act alone can create excitement. Although wasabi is unique to Japan, it is now known all over the world, and is one of the spices that represents this country.

Two types of wasabi appear at sushi restaurants; the type that is grated fresh at the counter, and the powdered type to which water is added to turn it into a paste. They are differentiated by calling the former "grated wasabi" (*suri wasabi* or *oroshi wasabi*) and the latter "wasabi paste" (*neri wasabi*). There's also a type of wasabi that comes in a tube. It's often said that the quality of wasabi varies greatly. This is because even if it's called wasabi, the quality can differ a lot depending on where it's from, the variety, and other factors. The variety held to be of the best quality is one called Mazuma, which is grown in places such as Izu Amagi and Gotenba in Shizuoka Prefecture, and Hotaka in Nagano Prefecture. Wasabi is grown in two ways. The type called "field wasabi" (*hatake wasabi*) is grown in fields, and the one called "marsh wasabi" (*sawa wasabi*) is grown in next to streams and ponds. The type used in sushi restaurants is marsh wasabi (see below), of which there are two varieties: Mazuma and Misho. The Misho variety is relatively easy to cultivate and is grown on a large scale, but the Mazuma variety is hard to cultivate and is not grown on a large scale. It grows slowly, at a rate of about 1 inch (3 cm) a year, and it takes eighteen months to three years from the time it is planted to the time it can be harvested. It takes one and a half times longer than the Misho variety to grow. In order to cultivate the Mazuma variety, terraced fields are used, and it's important to have a close source of clean water that can be kept at below 59°F (15°C) even in summer, as well as a large amount of oxygen. Mazuma wasabi is harvested by hand. Large rhizomes with small bumps are regarded as a sign of good quality. Wasabi should be firm, have a lot of body when grated, a refined spiciness and refreshing aroma.

What is wasabi?

Wasabi belongs to the Brassicaceae or mustard family, as do daikon radish and komatsuna greens. The type of wasabi that is grated fresh at sushi restaurants is usually marsh wasabi (*sawa wasabi*), which is grown in fields next to clean streams. The rhizomes are bumpy, dark green in color and thick. Because marsh wasabi has a superior spiciness and aroma, it is sold at very high prices.

The Composition of Wasabi

When wasabi is grated and its structure is broken down, enzymes go to work to produce a spicy component. A very fine-toothed grater such as one made with shark skin is usually used to grate wasabi, to break down its structure thoroughly, so that the enzymes can do their job and bring out the spicy flavor.

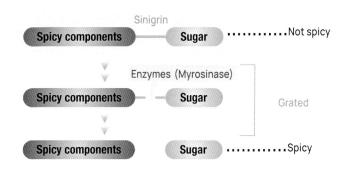

When wasabi has just been grated, those enzymes haven't yet had the time to work so it isn't very spicy. If grated wasabi is left for a while it will become spicier, but if it's left for too long the spicy components will dissipate. For this reason, it's best to grate only as much wasabi as needed each time in order to maximize the spiciness and aroma. If it is grated in advance, a small bowl called a *sabichoko* is placed over it.

The spicy component of wasabi also has antibacterial qualities. Research has shown that it is especially effective against *Vibrio parahaemolyticus*, a bacterium that originates in fish.

Citrus Fruit

Citrus Fruit
(*Kankitsu*)

Citrus fruit such as *sudachi*, *yuzu* and *kabosu* are garnishes that are essential to fish dishes in Japanese cooking. When they are squeezed over white fish such as sea bream or flounder, octopus and squid, as well as silver-skinned fish such as sardines, the acidity of the citrus enhances the individual flavors of the fish in a refreshing manner.

When it comes to the acidic ingredients for sushi, citrus juice is right up there with vinegar. From the time when sushi went from a food that mainly used cooked seafood toppings to one that used raw toppings, the use of citrus juice and zest increased.

The acidity of citrus fruit comes from citric acid. The acidity of vinegar comes from acetic acid. Both are organic acids. As the name indicates, organic acids are acidic, with a pH value of 7 and below. Organic acids prevent oxidation and the growth of bacteria. However, citrus fruits are used with sushi for their refreshing aroma and flavor rather than for their preservative qualities.

Citrus fruit used for sushi

The list below gives the main citrus fruits used with sushi, the principal regions where they are grown, and their season.

Yuzu
Kochi and Tokushima prefectures
October to December

Sudachi
Tokushima Prefecture
September

Kabosu
Oita Prefecture
September

Ginger Marinated with Sweet Vinegar

Thinly sliced ginger pickled in sweet vinegar is called *gari*. It performs the same function as green tea, in that it eliminates the taste of the previous sushi from the mouth when you are eating different types of sushi, and refreshes the taste buds.

The reason why sushi ginger is called *gari* is thought to be because of the crunchy sound it makes when its eaten or sliced. This sound is conveyed in Japanese by the phrase *gari gari*. The gari gari sound occurs because ginger is hard with a lot of fibers. The ginger plant is made up of leaves, stems and roots, as are other plants, but the fibrous part that is eaten and turned into sushi ginger is the underground root.

The name of ginger changes depending on when it's harvested and what time of year it is. Ginger (*shoga*) and new ginger (*shin shoga*) are the most common. The first type in the previous sentence is harvested in the fall, stored for more than two months and then sold on the market year round. New ginger is ginger that has just been harvested. It has a pale color all over, and the leaf bases are pink. It is shipped out between May and August only. New ginger is less fibrous than regular ginger, and more tender. Another type of ginger, sold in early summer with its leaves on, is called yanaka ginger (*yanaka shoga*). It is usually pickled in sweet vinegar and served with grilled fish as a garnish called *hajikami*. In the summer, some sushi restaurants serve thinly sliced hajikami instead of regular sushi ginger to highlight the season.

The properties of ginger

The spicy flavor components of ginger, such as zingerone and shogaol, are said to reduce the "fishy" taste of fish. Also, research shows that blood flow in the body increases after eating ginger. This is why it's been said since olden times that eating ginger warms you up. The spicy components are also believed to increase the appetite.

1 For every 9 lbs (4 kg) of new ginger, use a vinegar seasoning made with 1 gallon (3.8 liters) of vinegar, 3¼ lbs (1.5 kg) of sugar and 1 cup (300 g) of salt. The gari sushi ginger at Sushi Takahashi is made with new ginger. The ginger is sliced thinly, and put into boiling water.

2 When the water comes back to a boil, the ginger is removed.

3 The ginger is drained into a colander.

4 The ginger is spread out on a flat sieve.

5 The ginger is squeezed out well while it's still hot and put into the vinegar mixture for half to a whole day.

Before the ginger is pickled

After the ginger is pickled

The Tamagoyaki Omelet

玉子焼き

Japanese Omelet
(*Tamagoyaki*)

Tamagoyaki, the classic Japanese omelet, is one of the essential elements of Edomae (traditional Tokyo-style) sushi. As it's difficult make well, it is often said "If you eat the tamagoyaki you can tell how good a sushi restaurant is." Although some sushi restaurants buy their tamagoyaki from specialists, making your own tamagoyaki following your own methods is really part of what it means to be a true Edomae sushi chef.

The tamagoyaki served at sushi restaurants varies from place to place, and comes in different flavors. You could say it's the one sushi topping that really shows the philosophy of each restaurant, from the way it's flavored to the way it's cooked, including the decision as to whether or not to bring in readymade tamagoyaki from a specialist or not. Most tamagoyaki are cooked to be thick, but they can be divided into two main types—those that contain ground fish or seafood, and those that don't.

The tamagoyaki found in Edomae (traditional Tokyo-style) sushi used to be puffy and soft and contained ground seafood. Tamagoyaki without ground seafood is said to have originated in general Japanese restaurants rather than sushi restaurants. This type of fishless tamagoyaki has only become prevalent at sushi restaurants in recent times.

Both types of tamagoyaki are made in square pans, but whether the egg mixture is cooked a little at a time in layers and rolled while it's being made, or made in one go without rolling it, depends on each restaurant.

Sushi Takahashi makes the type of tamagoyaki with ground seafood in it. Our recipe is something we have achieved after many years of trial and error. The ground seafood used in our tamagoyaki is shrimp. Instead of mincing it, we turn it into a kind of liquid in a blender and mix it with egg to use as the base. We pour it into a square tamagoyaki pan and cook it with two heat sources, top and bottom, until we have a puffy finish. Because we use two heat sources, the tamagoyaki cooks up differently on the top and the bottom—the top has a pudding-like consistency, and the bottom has a cake-like consistency. The two differently textured layers make a irresistible match.

1 Put sake, granulated sugar and salt in a pan and bring it to a boil, then add the small shrimp. Put this in a blender and liquefy it (we'll call this the shrimp liquid from here on). Break the eggs into a bowl, add granulated sugar, salt, kombu seaweed dashi stock, mirin and sake, and mix.

2 Add the shrimp liquid to the egg liquid and mix again.

3 Put a grill rack on top of a gas cooker. Over a low flame, spread oil over a square tamagoyaki pan using a paper towel.

4 Pour the egg mixture into the pan little by little. As shown in the photo, you may also place cooking chopsticks between the pan and the grill rack to keep the pan at optimum distance from the heat.

5 Fill the tamagoyaki pan with the egg mixture. If any bubbles form on the surface, pop them with a gas torch. Turn the gas cooker flame down very low.

6 Arrange things so you can put a grill rack about 8 inches (20 cm) above the top of the pan. Place the hot charcoal on top of the grill rack. The important thing here is the distance between the pan and each heat source – the flame of the gas burner and the charcoal above. At Sushi Takahashi this is controlled by putting cooking chopsticks on the grill rack below, and having props such as bricks or other kitchen equipment on both sides to hold the grill rack at the correct distance. The tamagoyaki is cooked like this for 30 to 45 minutes.

If you look carefully at a tamagoyaki from Sushi Takahashi, you'll see there are two layers. This is because of the two different heat sources used for the top and bottom.

Methods of Cooking at a Sushi Restaurant

The two types of cooking done with heat at a sushi restaurant are wet cooking or simmering, and dry cooking, in other words, grilling or pan-frying. Simmering is done with conger eel, octopus, mantis shrimp and so on. Dry cooking is used for tamagoyaki (see page 138), or, for example, when grilling simmered conger eel slightly to give it a nuttiness. Some sushi restaurants these days are putting increasing emphasis on cooked appetizers, but the cooking that traditionally takes place at a sushi restaurant is for the preparation of sushi toppings. Chefs are always thinking of how the food will match up with the sushi rice as they cook it.

Making a tamagoyaki omelet in the style of Sushi Takahashi

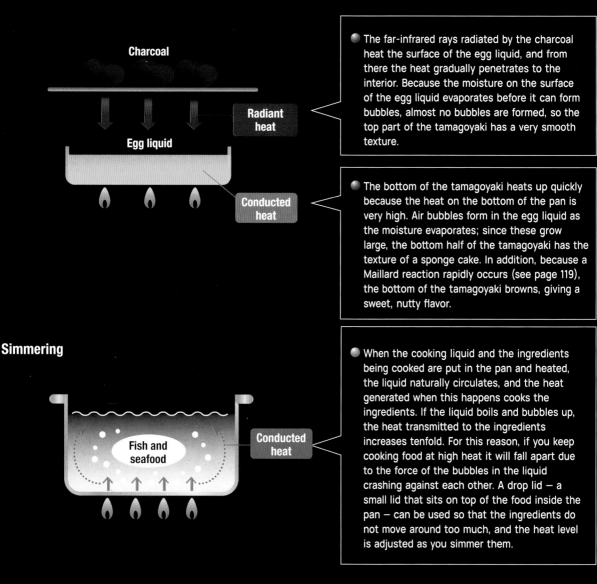

Charcoal

Radiant heat

Egg liquid

Conducted heat

● The far-infrared rays radiated by the charcoal heat the surface of the egg liquid, and from there the heat gradually penetrates to the interior. Because the moisture on the surface of the egg liquid evaporates before it can form bubbles, almost no bubbles are formed, so the top part of the tamagoyaki has a very smooth texture.

● The bottom of the tamagoyaki heats up quickly because the heat on the bottom of the pan is very high. Air bubbles form in the egg liquid as the moisture evaporates; since these grow large, the bottom half of the tamagoyaki has the texture of a sponge cake. In addition, because a Maillard reaction rapidly occurs (see page 119), the bottom of the tamagoyaki browns, giving a sweet, nutty flavor.

Simmering

Fish and seafood

Conducted heat

● When the cooking liquid and the ingredients being cooked are put in the pan and heated, the liquid naturally circulates, and the heat generated when this happens cooks the ingredients. If the liquid boils and bubbles up, the heat transmitted to the ingredients increases tenfold. For this reason, if you keep cooking food at high heat it will fall apart due to the force of the bubbles in the liquid crashing against each other. A drop lid – a small lid that sits on top of the food inside the pan – can be used so that the ingredients do not move around too much, and the heat level is adjusted as you simmer them.

Charcoal Grilling

When charcoal grilling, 80 percent of the heat transmitted from charcoal is radiant heat from infrared rays. Compared to the infrared rays released by gas heat, charcoal releases longer rays, in other words the amount of far-infrared rays is higher. When food is cooked with far-infrared rays it browns faster, and the surface becomes dry and crisp. In addition, the surface temperature of charcoal is high, 1470 to 2192°F (800 to 1200°C), which is another reason why charcoal grilling produces nuttier, crispier results.

Gas cooking (heat source: gas)

A gas cooker generates heat with a chemical reaction between the gas and the oxygen in the atmosphere. If there is enough oxygen and the gas burns off completely, the flames are blue, and if there isn't enough oxygen and the gas doesn't burn off completely the flames become red. Due to the convection heat of the air, heat is conducted to the sides of the pan as well as the bottom. The heat transmission rate of gas is about 40 percent.

Induction cooking (heat source: electricity)

Induction cookers are also called IH (induction heating) cookers. While gas cookers transmit heat to the pan via the hot air around the flames, induction cookers heat the bottom of the pan directly, transmitting heat from the bottom of the pan to the interior. For this reason the heat transmission rate of induction heating is about twice that of gas, around 80 to 90 percent.

Cooking Eggs

Eggs started to be widely eaten by the Japanese in the nineteenth century. Even back then, eggs were so popular that a cookbook with more than a hundred egg recipes appeared. There are many egg recipes around the world too — the egg is an ingredient with characteristics that are easy to manipulate in many ways. At sushi restaurants not only are they used to make tamagoyaki omelets, they're also used to make the savory egg custard known as *chawanmushi*.

The structure of an egg

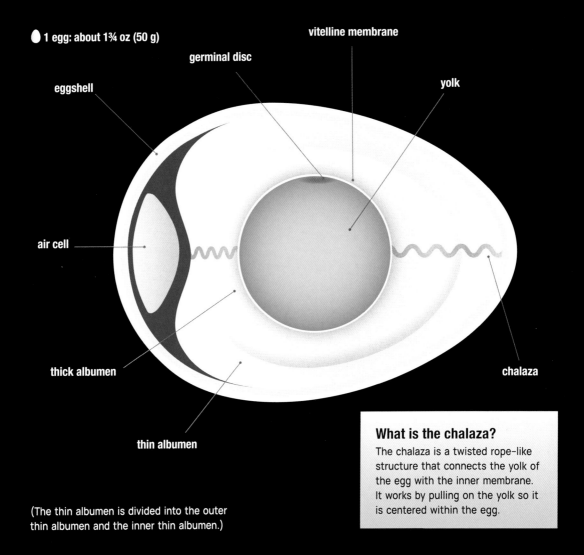

1 egg: about 1¾ oz (50 g)

germinal disc

vitelline membrane

eggshell

yolk

air cell

thick albumen

chalaza

thin albumen

(The thin albumen is divided into the outer thin albumen and the inner thin albumen.)

What is the chalaza?

The chalaza is a twisted rope-like structure that connects the yolk of the egg with the inner membrane. It works by pulling on the yolk so it is centered within the egg.

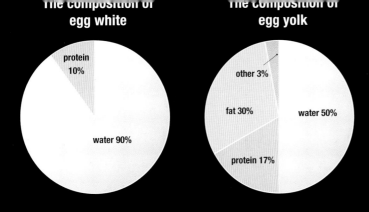

The composition of egg white

protein 10%

water 90%

The composition of egg yolk

other 3%

fat 30%

water 50%

protein 17%

Although the white of the egg contains 90 percent water and no fat, the yolk contains fat, of which 20 percent is a substance called lecithin. This lecithin can emulsify oil and water, which usually do not mix together. When an egg is beaten it becomes a liquid mixture of the yolk and white. The reason why dashi stock can be incorporated into this mixture is because of the emulsifying properties of lecithin.

Egg Characteristics 1

Egg can be mixed with dashi stock

Egg coagulates when heated. We take advantage of this by mixing dashi stock and other liquids with egg to make *dashimaki tamago* omelet, *chawanmushi* savory egg custard and other egg dishes. An egg has a structure where the yolk and white are enclosed in the capsule of the egg shell (see graphic on the facing page). The yolk and white have different compositions, and different characteristics too. Since elements with different characteristics are mixed together, the way they are mixed is important. The way heat is conducted through the thick and thin parts of the egg white (the albumen) differ, so they have to be mixed evenly or they will cook unevenly, and the egg will not brown evenly. At Sushi Takahashi we use a whisk and mix the egg with a cutting motion, so as not to incorporate any air into the egg white so that the egg mixture does not inflate more than is necessary when cooked. By passing the mixture through a sieve it becomes more evenly mixed, and the cooked result becomes beautifully even

Egg to dashi-stock ratio

Dashimaki tamago omelet   Egg 3 : Dashi 1
Chawanmushi egg custard   Egg 1 : Dashi 3

The egg white becomes foamy

Egg Characteristics 2

The type of sponge cake–like *atsuyaki tamago* (thick omelet) where egg is combined with shrimp or white fish paste and cooked slowly to a fluffy light finish, is a dish that has inherited Edo-period traditions. In general it is made by adding sugar, salt and *yamaimo* yam as a binder to the egg and shrimp or fish paste. The sugar is superfine sugar, or mirin can be used instead, and sometimes the yam is omitted. Each sushi restaurant has their own carefully thought-out formula for atsuyaki tamago. Some places add a layer of foamy meringue to the atsuyaki tamago, serving it as a kind of dessert after a sushi meal.

Egg white can be whipped until foamy. Water alone does not become foamy when it's whipped. Water molecules bond together strongly and pull towards each other so that they do not become separated. Even if air gets between the molecules, that bonding power pops any air bubbles. Egg white consists of protein dissolved in water. When protein is present the bonds between the molecules weaken, allowing air to get in. A film of protein forms around the air bubbles, so the bubbles do not break down easily. This is why egg white holds in air bubbles when whipped, and you can make a stable foam with it.

Egg hardens with heat

Egg Characteristics 3

Egg white hardens when heated because of the nature of protein. The Chinese characters 蛋白 that are used to represent the word "protein" in Japanese mean "egg" and "white substance"—in other words, the term "egg white" is synonymous with protein. Protein has a complex structure, and when it is heated, its structure changes (this change is called denaturation), which is why it hardens.

As described on the facing page, the ways the white and yolk of an egg harden differ depending on the heating temperature.

When the egg mixture hits the tamagoyaki pan and makes a sizzling sound, the surface of the pan is around 300°F (150°C).

Fresh eggs and old eggs

The fresher the egg, the more thick albumen (egg white) it has, so when the shell of a fresh egg is cracked open, both the yolk and the white are plump and rounded. Freshly laid eggs are somewhat on the alkaline side, but the older the egg gets the more strongly alkaline it becomes. The egg white has amino acids that contain sulfur; when sulfur is heated, it breaks down and releases a compound called hydrogen sulfide. This is why boiled eggs sometimes smell like sulfur hot springs. The reason a yolk turns dark when an egg is boiled for a long time is because the iron that is in it bonds with the hydrogen sulfide in the white and turns into a dark green compound called iron sulfide.

Hydrogen sulfide is released more easily when the egg becomes more alkaline, so old eggs release it more than fresh eggs, and their yolks become dark.

In addition, when an egg becomes more alkaline, the amount of white that adheres closely to the inside membrane of the shell lessens, so boiled eggs become easier to peel.

The relationship between the solidification of the whites and yolks of eggs

Temperature	The state of the egg white*	The state of the egg yolk
131°F (55°C)	Liquid, transparent, almost no change	No change
135°F (57°C)	Liquid, turning white	No change
138°F (59°C)	Translucent white jellylike state	No change
140°F (60°C)	Translucent white jellylike state	No change
144°F (62°C)	Semi-translucent milky jellylike state	No change
145°F (63°C)	Semi-translucent milky jellylike state	A little sticky, but almost no change
149°F (65°C)	Semi-translucent white jellylike state; wobbly	Sticky and soft, gluelike consistency
154°F (68°C)	White jellylike state, partially hardened	Sticky, stiff, gluelike consistency; almost soft set
158°F (70°C)	Semi-soft and forms a mass, but still partially liquid	Sticky, gluelike consistency; soft set
167°F (75°C)	Semi-soft and forms a mass; no liquid parts	Springy, rubberlike, soft set; color is slightly pale
176°F (80°C)	Totally hardened; hard	Still a little sticky, but falls apart; pale yellow color
185°F (85°C)	Totally hardened; hard	Not much stickiness or resilience; falls apart easily; whiter color

* Records the changes when the egg white and yolk are separated, and 5 grams of each are put into test tubes and cooked in 131°F to 185°F (55°C to 85°C) water for 8 minutes.

From Sato, Hidemi: *The Science of Heat that Creates Taste*, Shibata Shoten

Oboro Ground Fish Paste

The paste known in Japanese as *oboro* is made by cooking white fish, such as cod or shrimp, in a pan until it forms fine granules. This paste has been made since the Edo period as a sushi topping or filling, and was indispensable for decorative sushi.

おぼろ

Ground Fish
Paste
(*Oboro*)

White fish that is low in fat, or shrimp, is usually used to make oboro. In the olden days, the type of seafood used to make oboro was said to show the status of the establishment, and shrimp was held to be the highest-grade ingredient. Boiled shrimp changes color naturally and gives a light pink hue to the oboro. Oboro is used in Edomae (traditional Tokyo-style) sushi in a layer between the fish and the sushi rice; it goes well with fish such as halfbeak or young seabream.

The fibers in white fish and shrimp are thick and loose, so they fall apart easily when heated. The fish or shrimp is turned into a paste, combined with seasonings and cooked slowly while constantly stirring. Although it depends on the heat level, it usually takes about twenty minutes or more to cook the paste until it turns into a finely grained oboro. Since the oboro made with cod is white, it is sometimes colored with red food coloring. Shrimp has an attractive pale pink color as is.

At Sushi Takahashi, we add egg to the shrimp-paste base to make our oboro. We also make egg yolk vinegar oboro, another old-style Edomae cooked item. This is made by mixing vinegar with an egg mixture that is heavy on yolk; when the protein in the egg liquid has transformed because of the acid in the vinegar (see step 2, opposite), it is cooked in a pan until it forms a very fine grainy mixture. It becomes a very pretty yellow oboro, which we serve with *kasugo* (young sea bream) sushi.

Shrimp oboro

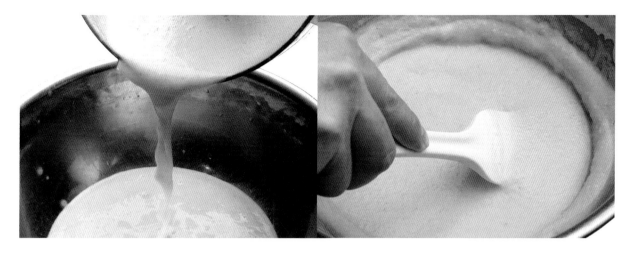

1 Put sake, salt and granulated sugar into a pan and bring to a boil. Add the whole shrimp until they are just cooked through. Take off the heat, liquefy in a blender, and transfer the mixture to a bowl.

2 Place the bowl in a water bath heated to about 176°F (80°C), and stir with a spatula. When the proteins in the shrimp start to harden and you feel resistance when you stir, put the mixture into a pan and add the egg yolk. Mix with five cooking chopsticks held together (see facing page), and keep cooking until the mixture forms fine grains.

Egg yolk vinegar oboro

Put egg yolks, whole eggs, sugar and vinegar into a bowl. Place the bowl in a water bath heated to about 176°F (80°C) and stir with a spatula. The protein in the egg will change because of the acid in the vinegar, and the mixture will start to harden, as seen in the photograph. When the mixture becomes lumpy transfer it to a pan. Keep cooking the mixture over low heat, while stirring it with five cooking chopsticks held together (see facing page), until it forms fine grains.

Dried Gourd Strips

The dried gourd strips known as *kanpyo* in Japanese are often used as a part of the filling for *norimaki* sushi rolls. Even though it's not a fish or seafood, it is an indispensable ingredient in Edomae (traditional Tokyo-style) sushi. In a sushi roll, the aroma of the nori seaweed, the sweetness of the kanpyo, and the acidity of the sushi rice come together as one, creating the perfect finale to your sushi restaurant meal.

かんぴょう

Dried Gourd
Strips
(*Kanpyo*)

Kanpyo is made by drying thin strips of the *yugao* gourd. Around 90 percent of the domestic production of kanpyo comes from Tochigi Prefecture. Good quality kanpyo is white in color with a sheen, and is thick and wide with a sweet scent. Most of the kanpyo available on the market has been treated with sulfurous acid (also used to preserve wine) to preserve and bleach it. Unbleached kanpyo is not generally available to buy. When the kanpyo is parboiled (soaked in water for about 5 minutes and boiled for 10 minutes) the sulfurous acid goes down to about one thirtieth of its original amount.

Kanpyo is rubbed with salt before it's soaked in water, which helps the fiber break down faster. It also makes the kanpyo absorb liquid better, so that seasonings can penetrate it more easily.

The yugao gourd is harvested in July to August when it has a moisture content of about 95 percent.

The gourd is cut into ropes 2-3 millimeters thick.

The gourd ropes are dried in the sun. The moisture content goes down to 20-30 percent.

(Photo credit: Tochigi Prefecture Rural Development Division)

Preparing kanpyo gourd

1 Soak the kanpyo strips in water overnight. They will absorb the water and swell to about 2.5 times their original weight. Drain off the water, add salt (about 20% of the weight of the kanpyo) to the bowl and massage the kanpyo using a grasping motion until it is wilted.

2 Rinse the kanpyo well in water, and wring it out well. Put some water in a pan, add the wrung out kanpyo strips, and heat. As they cook, add more water two or three times until the kanpyo strips are translucent and you can rip them with your hands. Drain into a colander and wring out well.

3 Put regular sugar, coarse or granulated sugar (*zarame,*) and soy sauce into a pan in a 3:3:2 ratio and bring to a boil. (With just regular sugar, the flavor would be too sweet; the addition of coarse or granulated sugar makes the taste milder.)

CHAPTER 3

THE ART OF SUSHI:
SHAPING, SLICING AND PRESENTATION

Shaping the Sushi

The most flamboyant part of making sushi is to shape it. The chef stands in front of the customer, forms the sushi and hands it to them. The sushi is formed to be quite airy so that the customer can carry it to their mouth without it crumbling, but once it's put in the mouth it should fall apart gently. In order for the chef to be able to make beautifully formed sushi time and time again, they must pay the utmost attention to every detail of the work.

To stand in the *tsukeba*—the area behind the sushi counter—and to show off one's sushi-making skills in front of the customer is one of the highlights of the sushi-making process for a chef. The customer watches the chef's every movement, filled with anticipation for what's to come.

Each sushi chef has their own way of making sushi, but they all have the aim of making well-formed and beautiful sushi as quickly and smoothly as possible. But as we have seen, even only it takes a few seconds to form each sushi roll, there are hours of preparation steps behind each piece.

Also bear in mind that the sushi chef does not just make one piece of sushi. In one session they make tens or hundreds of pieces of sushi from a variety of toppings, all with the same size and shape. For this reason it's important for a sushi chef to work on their core strength to maintain good sushi-making form, much like an athlete!

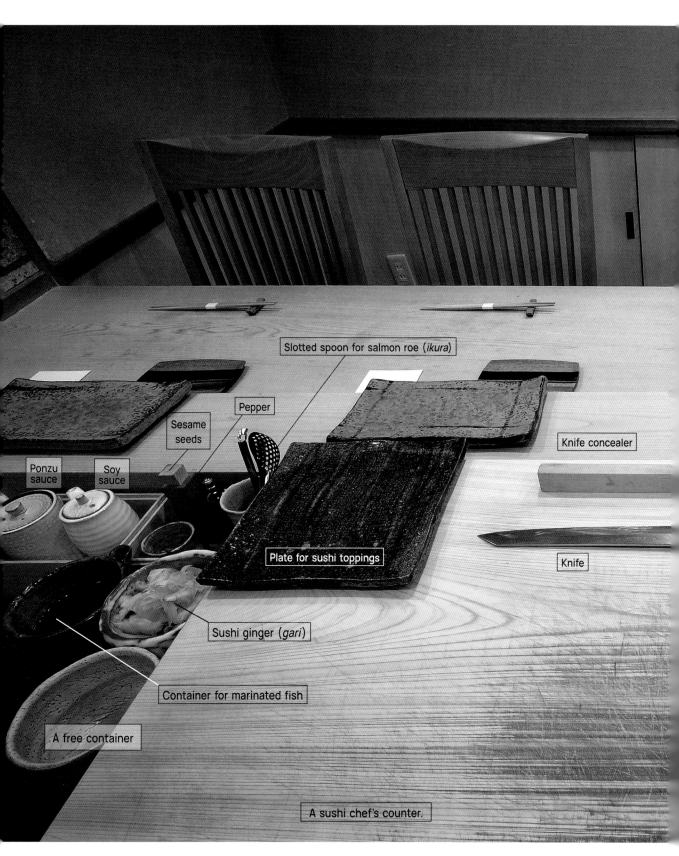

Slotted spoon for salmon roe (*ikura*)

Pepper

Sesame
seeds

Knife concealer

Ponzu
sauce

Soy
sauce

Plate for sushi toppings

Knife

Sushi ginger (*gari*)

Container for marinated fish

A free container

A sushi chef's counter.

Nitsume sauce

Vinegar for the hands

Tamagoyaki

Nikiri sauce

Sushi rice

Long cooking
chopsticks

Wasabi

The Ohitsu Wooden Rice Container

An *ohitsu* is a container traditionally used to keep rice warm. It maintains the temperature of sushi rice at body temperature. Sushi restaurants mainly use wooden ohitsu, which not only maintain the temperature of the rice but prevent it from drying out too. The aroma imparted by the wood of the container is also a plus.

In order to maintain the temperature of the rice, sushi restaurants often use a wooden container called an ohitsu. The container is also called an *ohachi*, and its formal name is *meshibitsu*. The word *hitsu* means a container with a lid; there are also wooden lidded containers for storing uncooked rice called *komebitsu*.

Although there are some restaurants who put a large amount of sushi rice in an ohitsu and then put the ohitsu in an insulating straw basket called a *warauzumi*, these days many chefs first put the sushi rice in a rice cooker with a keep-warm function, and then transfer as much rice as is needed at one time to an ohitsu, placing the ohitsu where they can reach it when they are making sushi.

Sushi restaurants usually use ohitsu made of Japanese cypress (*hinoki*) or cryptomeria (*sugi*) wood. In addition to the previously mentioned functions of keeping the rice warm, stopping it from drying out and imparting a pleasant fragrance, an ohitsu also looks good on a wooden counter. For all of these reasons, a wooden ohitsu is preferred.

How to Care for an Ohitsu

A new ohitsu A brand new ohitsu has a distinctive aroma. Fill the new ohitsu with boiling water to which 2 to 3 sake cups of vinegar have been added and leave to soak for 2 to 3 hours. Then wash the ohitsu in water and wipe dry. Any aroma and bitterness that came from the wood should be gone.

Everyday care Always wipe the inside of the ohitsu with a wrung-out kitchen towel before using it. After use, wash it with a neutral dishwashing detergent if needed, and leave to dry out completely in a shady location. If it is exposed to direct sunlight the wood will shrink rapidly. Occasionally, a resin that naturally occurs in wood will rise to the surface. This is harmless to humans, but if it bothers you, wipe it off with denatured alcohol.

Storing an ohitsu When the ohitsu needs to be stored for a while because it's not in use, wrap it in paper or a kitchen towel before storing. The storage location should have a stable temperature and low humidity. Do not store the ohitsu with the lid on; wrap the lid separately.

Removing mold Should any mold grow on the ohitsu while it's being used, scrub it off lightly with bicarbonate of soda or salt. Both are abrasive, so if you rub too hard, the soft part of the wood will get shaved off and the surface of the ohitsu will become rough.

Removing odors If the ohitsu develops an odor that bothers you, treat it as you did when it was brand new by filling it with boiling water and 2 to 3 sake cups of vinegar, and leaving it for 2 to 3 hours. Wash in water and wipe dry afterwards.

If the metal rings become loose If the wood dries out, the metal rings (*taga*) holding the ohitsu together may come off. If so, push them back to their original positions with your hands, hold them in place while you fill the ohitsu with water, and wait for the wood to absorb the water and swell up. If the rings are still too loose, position them a bit higher so they fit better, fill the ohitsu with water again and wait for the wood to swell up.

How the temperature of the sushi rice changes in an ohitsu

Sushi Takahashi first puts the rice in a insulated thermal container, then transfers it one heaping rice bowl at a time into a small ohitsu positioned to the right of the chef's workstation. This is the amount that gets used up within about 5 minutes. The graph shows the changes in temperature of the rice within the ohitsu, as measured by the editorial staff. When the rice has just been transferred to the ohitsu, its surface temperature is about 109°F (43°C). When the lid is placed on it, heat is transmitted from the interior of the rice to the surface, raising the temperature slightly. The ohitsu has such superior thermal qualities that it can maintain the temperature of the rice at above 104°F (40°C) for 20 minutes.

How the temperature of the rice is measured

where the temperature is measured

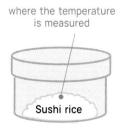

Sushi rice

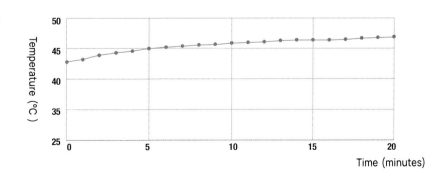

* As measured by the editorial staff. The lid of the ohitsu was kept closed, and opened only to measure the temperature.

Slicing the Toppings

The act of slicing larger blocks of fish (*saku*) to the size that fits the topping is called *kiritsuke*. If the slices are too big or too small in relation to the sushi rice they don't look good, so the beauty of each piece of sushi is determined by the kiritsuke. In principle the fish is sliced diagonally, against its grain. Just before it's sliced all the way through, the diagonally placed knife blade is turned so that it's perpendicular to the cutting board. This act is called to "turn the knife" or to "make the knife do its work." Since the blade is sharpened on only one side, the cut surface of the sushi has a nice sharp edge, which makes it look beautiful.

Of course there is more to consider than simply creating a nice appearance. Since each fish differs—even the same type of fish can be different depending on the season or the region it came from—it's necessary to change the cut depending on the fish. The chef must judge how fatty the fish is, how tender it is and so on, simply by looking or touching, and slice it more thickly, thinly, or put some hidden cuts in it as he thinks necessary. For example, lean skipjack tuna caught early in the season is sliced thickly, while fatty late-season skipjack tuna is sliced on the thin side. These are the moments when the experience and instincts of the sushi chef come into play.

Slicing tuna

1 Insert the heel of a yanagiba knife (see page 24) against the grain of the tuna diagonally.

2 Pull the blade towards you; just before the blade has gone all the way through turn it perpendicular to the cutting board, and slice through.

Slicing gaper clam

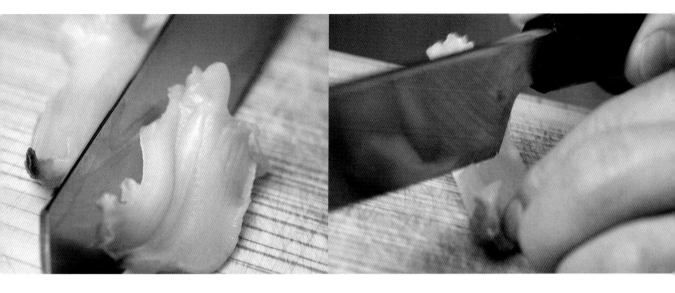

1 Slice the clam in half vertically, so that each piece has a bit of the red end part.

2 Make small crisscross cuts in the surface with the heel of the knife.

Slicing sea bream

1 Cut into the fish diagonally against the grain. This determines the thickness of the slice. Just before the blade has gone all the way through turn it perpendicular to the cutting board, and slice through.

2 Line up each slice depending on how many are needed.

The Movements for Shaping Sushi

To be able to shape sushi in a series of smooth movements, everything has to be in order in advance — this is known as the *mise en place*. Whether the chef can respond immediately when the customer places and order and quickly make sushi that tastes good and is well formed depends on the *mise en place*.

The necessary components for making the sushi — the sushi rice, toppings, the wasabi and so on — should always be placed in the same positions. A clean folded kitchen cloth is used to keep the work surface impeccable. The cloth is moistened with *temizu* vinegared water and wrung out tightly. Temizu consists of vinegar and water mixed in equal proportions and is used by the chef on his hands so that the rice does not stick to them. If the work surface gets oily or wet, it is wiped off right away. Since raw products are being handled, it is important to practice good hygiene.

The plate holding the wasabi is turned right-side up (it's kept upside down until the last moment to maintain the aroma) and the wrung-out and folded kitchen cloth is placed in front of the chef. The sliced sushi toppings are placed slightly to left of the chef. He is in position.

The chef puts a little temizu vinegared water on the tip of his right-hand middle fingers.

The middle fingers that were dipped in the vinegared water are placed on the palm of the left hand; the palms are held together to moisten them both.

The chef takes enough rice for one piece of sushi from the ohitsu container with his right hand – for most sushi rolls except for shrimp this would weigh 12 grams; for a gunkan roll (where the nori seaweed is wrapped around the sides of the rice ball and the toppings mounded on top) it would weigh 11 grams; and for shrimp it would weigh 8 grams. The rice is rolled in the hands to shape it lightly. At the same time he picks up the sushi topping with the thumb and forefinger of his left hand, and places it across the second joint of the fingers (see top picture overleaf).

With the sushi topping still held on the second joints of the left hand, the sushi rice is pressed with the middle, ring and little fingers of the right hand.

While the sushi rice is pressed with the right hand, the left hand is held in a stable position.

With the sushi rice still held in the right hand, the chef takes a little wasabi with the forefinger of that hand.

The wasabi is placed in the center of the topping held in the left hand.

The sushi rice is placed on the sushi topping. If there is too much rice, this is adjusted at this point.

The center of the sushi rice is pressed firmly with the thumb of the left hand. Then the index and middle fingers of the right hand are stretched out, and pressed on top of the rice.

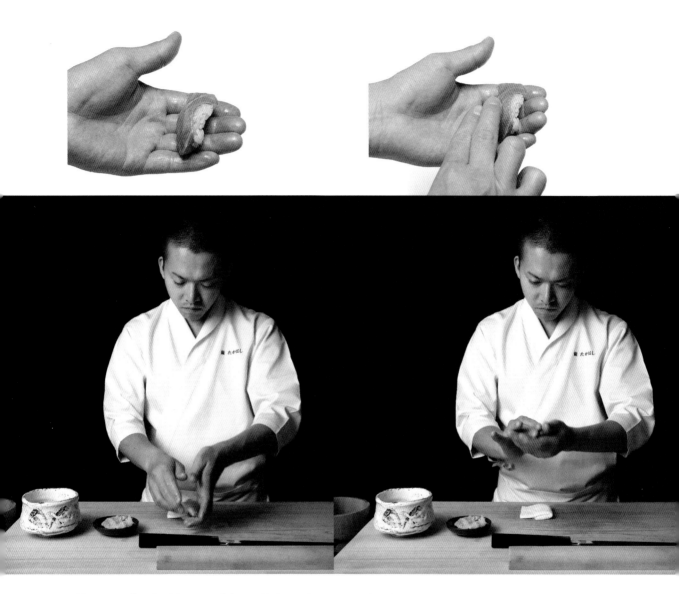

The sushi is pressed lightly with the straightened index and middle fingers of the right hand and rolled to the end of the fingers to flip it over, so the topping is now on top.

The index and middle fingers of the right hand are straightened out to press on top of the sushi topping. The rice is held lightly on both sides with the palm and fingers of the left hand.

The sushi is turned clockwise with the right hand.

The sushi is pressed on the left and right sides with the thumb and middle finger of the right hand.

The sushi is pressed on top with the index finger of the right hand.

The sushi is turned clockwise with the right hand.

The sushi is pressed on the left and right sides with the thumb and middle finger of the right hand.

Before the sushi is served to the customer, it's put on the cutting board to tidy up its shape.

The completed sushi piece, with air between the rice grains, none of which have been crushed, is ready to eat.

The Individuality of Sushi Makers

Sushi has crossed the oceans and its popularity has spread throughout the world, All kinds of colorful toppings have made their appearance thanks to the skills of various sushi chefs. However, even as sushi changes with the times, the traditional *nigirizushi* sushi balls and *makizushi* sushi rolls that typify the art of the Edomae (traditional Tokyo-style) chef still have a definitive presence.

Sushi shows the individuality of the maker. At Sushi Takahashi, chef Jun Takahashi puts the topping on the fingers of one hand, takes the sushi rice with his other hand, presses his hands together lightly and lovingly, and before you know it the sushi has been formed and is presented on the serving board. Although each piece is small, they are all beautifully formed. Even though they stay intact while waiting to be eaten, once they are put in the mouth, the rice falls apart instantly. Toppings such as fatty tuna (*otoro*) are presented on slightly warm sushi rice, while toppings with less fat, such as sea bream (*tai*) and olive flounder (*hirame*) are served on rice that is a little cooler. Chef Takahashi makes fine adjustments to such things as the temperature of the rice by positioning it carefully within the *ohitsu* container, and makes his sushi using instincts developed during his many years of experience. The distinctive quality and finish of the sushi he makes is memorable. This book showcases Chef Takahashi's "now," the place he has reached as a result of all his previous efforts. But he says his method may still evolve. This is because sushi is not just a matter of placing sliced fish onto a ball of rice, but a cuisine created through a melding of technique, knowledge and experience.

On the following pages, Chef Takahashi presents the different types of sushi he creates, with commentary in his own words.

Although making sushi is the simple task of putting a topping onto rice and shaping it, the personality of the maker is notably evident in the sushi's form, mouthfeel and taste. This is the attraction and the essence of sushi.

Toppings

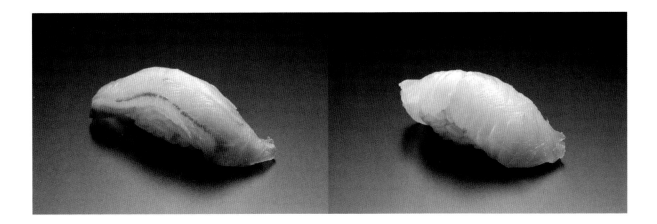

Sea Bream 鯛
Tai

From its impressive appearance to its beautiful coloring and deep flavor, *tai*, also known as *madai* or "true sea bream," is truly worthy of being called the king of fish. At Sushi Takahashi we only serve it in the early spring, from February to April. The *madai* in this period is a powerful fish, and when we get it in, it has a crunchy texture, but by aging it slowly its texture softens so that the fat permeates the flesh better and it melds well with the sushi rice when put in the mouth.

The way we age the fish is to first vacuum pack it with the head still on, and put it onto ice. The aging period differs depending on the size of the fish, but a 9 pound (4 kilo) fish is refrigerated for five to six days. Sea bream in season that has been aged has a sweet flavor. Although we put soy sauce on it when we serve it as sushi, when it is served alone as an appetizer it comes just with salt.

Olive Flounder 鮃
Hirame

The main white fish of the winter is the olive flounder (*hirame*). The *kan birame*—olive flounder caught in the cold season—has a nice amount of fat right under the skin, and has a wonderful aroma. It also has a distinct texture, a subtle sweetness and a deep flavor—it's a noble fish. Although it used to be caught in Tokyo Bay, you don't see them caught here anymore; instead, ones caught in Aomori Prefecture or around Joban in Fukushima Prefecture are often seen on the market.

When seen from above, the olive flounder has a black-skin side and a white-skin side, and each side has a different texture. The black side is thick, and the white side has a bit more fat. You can also get a lot of *engawa* tail-fin muscle from the white side too. Each sushi restaurant differs as to which side they prefer; here at Sushi Takahashi, we like the white side, and that's what we choose to buy. We get in halved fish with the head still intact, and hold it on ice in a styrofoam box for three to four days. Sometimes we also cure it in kombu seaweed.

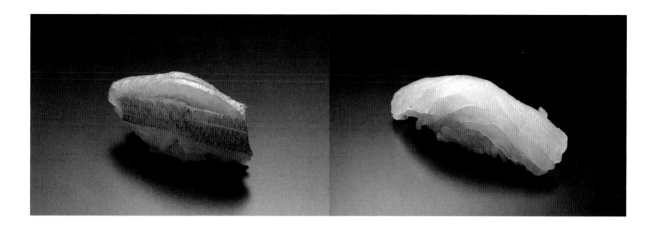

Young Sea Bream

Kasugo

The Japanese name of this fish contains the characters 春 "spring" and 子 "child," indicating that this fish is the younger, smaller member of the sea bream family, at about 6 inches (15 cm) long. Its pretty pink color as well as its name make this fish the harbinger of spring. Since the tender flesh is eaten with the skin intact, it is classified as a silver-skinned fish (*hikarimono*, see page 62) rather than as a white fish. Young sea bream must be fresh. It is broken down as soon as it's brought in, and boiling water is poured over the skin side to blanch it. Doing this means it can be eaten with the skin, and one can enjoy the aroma and taste of that skin. With its tender texture and clean taste, young sea bream is something I would like everyone to enjoy for its seasonality. It is served with some vinegar-flavored oboro under it.

Right-Eye Flounder

Karei

Right-eye flounder is a white fish that represents the summer season. Two types of this fish— *hoshigarei* and *makogarei*—are used for sushi. The catches of hoshigarei are so low that it's called a phantom fish. At Sushi Takahashi we mostly use makogarei, which is characterized by its firm flesh. Because it is so firm, we age it before it is used. To age it, we put it on ice in a styrofoam box with its head intact for three to four days. We cure it with kombu seaweed sometimes too.

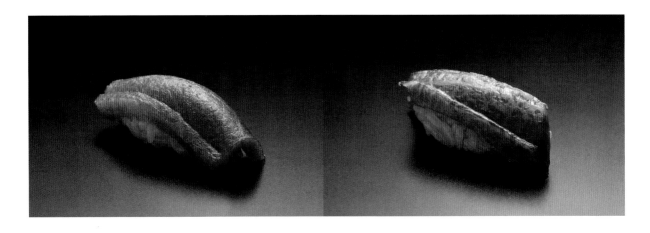

Medium Marbled Tuna Belly

Chutoro

Tuna is the star of Edomae (traditional Tokyo-style) sushi. Of the different cuts, medium fatty tuna (*chutoro*) has an attractive gradation between the lean red meat and the fat, and it melts smoothly in your mouth. Although it comes from different regions depending on the season, the best is the bluefin tuna caught in the waters around Japan from September to December. Their bodies are overflowing with power; they are aged in the refrigerator for about two weeks to bring out their umami. I believe that the quality of tuna is decided entirely on where it comes from and how it is aged. When buying tuna, I always consult a wholesaler I trust, and make my decision after discussing which one to buy and how long to age it. However, if the fish itself has no power, no amount of aging will make it taste good. I decide which ones to buy depending on the amount of moisture in the body, how firm it is, and how much fat is on it, but as a matter of fact I personally feel that a tuna that is a bit dull colored has more umami than one that is bright red.

Premium Marbled Tuna Belly

Otoro

Like marbled beef, tuna belly (*otoro*) has a high fat content, melts as soon as you put it in your mouth, and leaves a rich umami flavor afterwards. Although it is the most expensive type of sushi topping, the flavor and texture can vary depending on where it's cut from. There are parts that are very well marbled, parts with tendons, and parts in between. Everyone has different preferences, but I love customers to try the tendons, which are soft and tender. It's not possible to only get in a single type of tuna belly, however, so I cut up the blocks in advance so that I can easily serve the customer the cut that they prefer. The marbled parts have some texture so they are sliced thinly, and the tender parts are sliced more thickly. In order for the fat to melt nicely, I make the sushi with rice that is on the warm side.

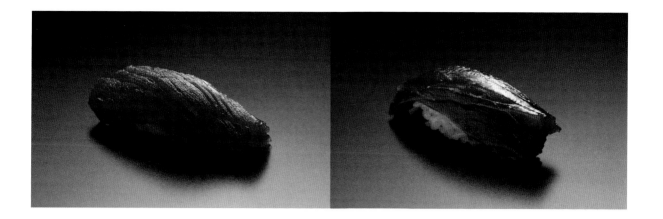

Lean Tuna

Akami or Maguro

Lean tuna (*akami* or *maguro*) used to be the type of tuna most associated with sushi, but these days it's had its spotlight taken away by *chutoro* and *otoro* (see facing page). However, the moist, finely textured meat and the deep flavor with a slight nuance of iron is something unique that you can't find in other cuts of fish. Lean tuna also totally differs in texture and flavor depending on where it's cut from, so I take account of this when preparing sushi. The part near the *chiai* (the dark red part that is not used for sushi) is tender and highly flavored, so I use it as is. The part near the chutoro has more tendons and texture, so I might marinate it (*zuke*, see next column). As with the other parts of the tuna, I believe lean tuna tastes better when it has a rather dull color rather than when it's bright red.

Marinated Tuna 漬け

Zuke

Zuke, tuna that is marinated in a *nikiri* sauce (see page 126) made of sake, mirin and soy sauce that have been brought to the boil and cooled, is a method born in the days when refrigeration was not available. However, it is still popular since it firms up the flesh of the fish, and adds umami. The part of the tuna that is made into zuke is the lean part (*akami*); we use the part that has a lot of tendons and texture. It is sliced just before it's made into sushi; the slices are marinated in the nikiri sauce for ten minutes, the sauce is wiped off lightly, and some of it is brushed onto the tuna after it has been placed on the sushi to finish. Although only marinated for ten minutes, the tuna develops a rich texture.

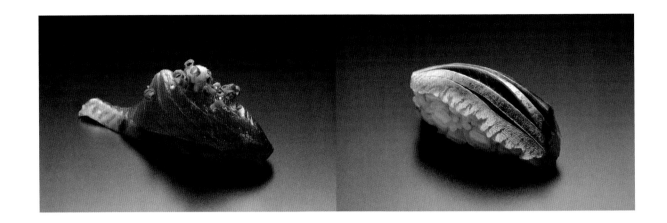

Skipjack Tuna

Katsuo

There are two seasons for skipjack tuna; spring, when the fish is called *hatsu katsuo* and fall, when it is called *modori katsuo*. The fall type have a strong aroma, and the spring type have a nice amount of fat and an aroma that is more delicate. Both are seared in the flames from burning straw before being made into sushi. Because of the delicate aroma of early skipjack tuna, it is just seared lightly so that the fragrance of the straw does not overwhelm it.

Skipjack tuna is delicious on its own, but when combined with its ideal partners, scallions and ginger, it becomes even more refreshing.

Sardine

Iwashi

The "true sardines" or *maiwashi* (Sardinops melanostictus; also known as Japanese pilchard), caught from summer to fall, especially those from Hokkaido, are packed with fat and are meltingly delicious, with a unique aroma and texture. Sardines must be fresh, and in principle should be used on the same day they are brought in. However when really good sardines caught at peak season are brought in, they are often transformed when they are left to rest for a day—the fat and the umami permeate the whole fish, and the flesh melts in your mouth.

Although sardines have a down-to-earth image, their price is steadily creeping up year by year.

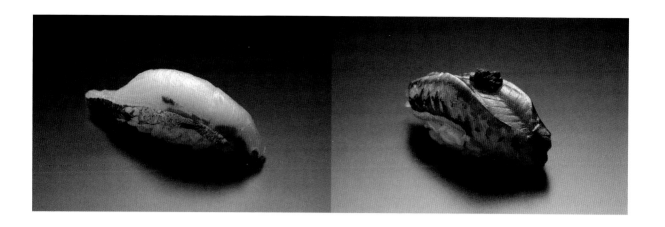

Striped Jack

Shima-aji

This is a beautiful sushi topping with a light pink color. The striped jack (also known as white trevally) caught in the wild in the summer is very scarce, so it's expensive.

High quality striped jack has a good amount of fat, with a moist texture and sweetness. We get the whole fish, and age it first. Although it is delicious when freshly caught, the flesh is too firm and doesn't meld well with the sushi rice. We find that aging it for a few days allows the flesh to settle down. Striped jack can suddenly go rancid during the aging process, so care has to be taken.

Horse Mackerel

Aji

The word *aji* also means "flavor" in Japanese, and there is a theory that this fish got its name because it tastes so good. Horse mackerel is in season in the summer, when its fat and umami both increase, and its flesh becomes meaty and firm. It has quite a long season, from mid-May to the beginning of fall, so we get it in from various regions. The ones available in the summer from Izumi in Kagoshima Prefecture are well packed with fat, so we prefer them over others.

Horse mackerel is one of the more popular sushi toppings. There are many people who don't like sushi made with silver-skinned fish but who like it made with horse mackerel. This may be because it has just the right amount of fat and a tender texture, both of which meld well with sushi rice. Horse mackerel is served with a garnish of scallions and ginger mixed together.

Gizzard Shad

小肌
Gizzard Shad
(*Kohada*)

Gizzard shad (*kohada*) is the sushi topping that most typifies Edomae (traditional Tokyo-style) sushi. Large gizzard shad, called *konoshiro* in Japanese, is a fish you would think was born to be a sushi topping—its flavor marries perfectly with vinegar, and it looks beautiful on top of a ball of rice. The character of each sushi restaurant can be seen by the way it cures gizzard shad in vinegar, and the decorative cuts they give it. The marination process varies depending on the size of the fish and how much fat it has, the ratio of salt and vinegar, and the curing time. If the gizzard shad is marinated for too long it will become too dry, and if it's not marinated long enough the vinegar and fish flesh won't become as one. Just-marinated fish is white in color and only tastes of vinegar, but it gradually becomes more yellow in color as the fat settles down. There is a moment when the acid leaves the flesh and is replaced by umami. The fish is usually marinated for about three days, but this can vary depending on its size, so it must be checked on daily.

Decorative cuts for gizzard shad

The cut surfaces of firm gizzard shad have sharply defined edges, making it possible to cut it in many decorative ways. At Sushi Takahashi we make three vertical cuts in it, as shown on the facing page.

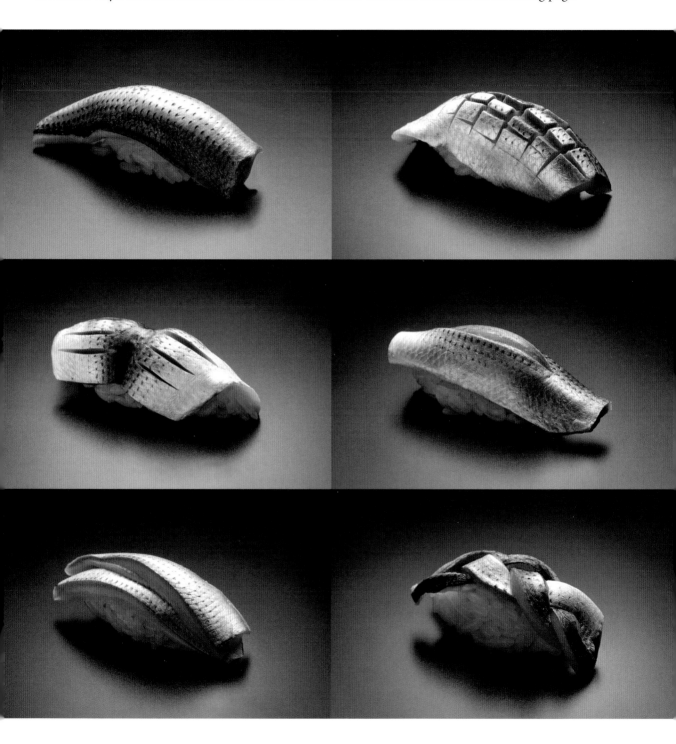

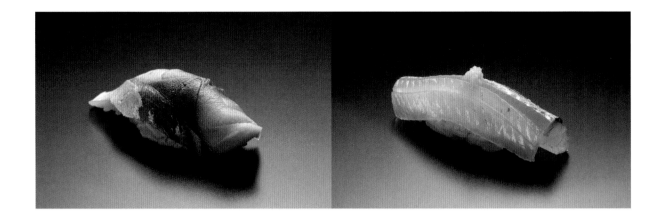

Mackerel

鯖

Saba

At Sushi Takahashi we serve mackerel cured with vinegar, sugar and salt, a style called *shimesaba* in Japanese. However, we only serve it in the winter months, when the mackerel has plenty of fat on it. First the mackerel is quickly broken down and cured with sugar. We sprinkle enough sugar to cover it completely, and leave for 30 minutes. We then salt it and leave it for 2 hours. Lastly we put it into vinegar: first, a diluted solution of vinegar and water to cure it slowly, and later on we put it in pure vinegar. Although it depends on the size of the fish, we usually put it in the diluted vinegar water for 3 minutes, and in the straight vinegar for 30 minutes. The mackerel is then wrapped in cling film and aluminum foil and refrigerated for 3 days. We check on how firm it's getting and how far the fat has permeated the flesh every day, but we can only tell how good or bad the result is after removing the breast bone, so we have to rely on our experience and instincts.

Halfbeak

細
魚

Sayori

With its refined-looking beautifully translucent flesh, its light-tasting yet rich texture on the tongue, and the indescribable flavor that fills your mouth, halfbeak is a great sushi topping. Since it comes into season at the end of winter, this fish is called a harbinger of spring. Because of its beautiful form and easy-to-handle flesh, sushi chefs in the olden days used it to make various decorative cuts.

Large halfbeak are called *kannuki*; at Sushi Takahashi that's all we use. Kannuki can be very expensive, but it's worth it for the deeper flavor. Incidentally, the word kannuki comes from the fact that the fish looks like a kannuki, a type of latch used to lock a double door. This fish is served with ginger on top; sometimes we also add egg yolk vinegar oboro (see page 148).

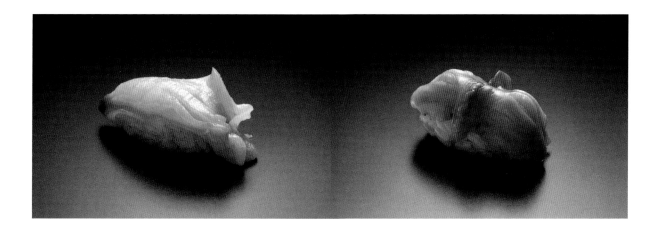

Gaper Clam

海松貝

Mirugai or Mirukui

This shellfish is also called the matsutake mushroom of the sea, comparing it to another highly prized food in Japan. Not only does it have a great texture, its aroma is wonderful. It has the firmest texture of all the shellfish used for sushi, so when we serve it we make the sushi rice quite firm too, so that it is well balanced with the texture of the topping. One gaper clam can yield to two to three portions for sushi. Recently, gaper clam is quite difficult to obtain, and it's become very expensive.

Ark Clam

赤貝

Akagai

With is beautiful appearance and rich aroma of the sea, ark clam, also known as red clam, is a popular sushi topping. At Sushi Takahashi we use the ones from the port town of Yuriage in Sendai, Miyagi Prefecture, which is famous for the quality of its ark clams.

To keep the clams as fresh as possible, we get in the whole clams rather than pre-shelled ones, and open them up one by one before making them into sushi. When you lightly insert a knife into the clam and bash it on the cutting board, the body forms a beautiful arched shape. The body is made into nigirizushi, and the *himo* or scallop mantle is used for sushi rolls.

Abalone

Awabi

The season for abalone is summer. When the abalone from southern Chiba Prefecture appear in late May, that signals the start of the season.

In order to bring out the umami, aroma and texture of the abalone to its fullest, we first simmer them in their shells. We then remove the bodies from the shells, and scrub then hard with a salt-laden scrubbing brush, to remove any bitterness. Then they are simmered again in the liquid that was used for the first round of simmering, adding water as needed, for four hours. Since abalone is gelatinous, if it is left in the simmering liquid to become cold it will harden, so it should be made into sushi as soon as it is cool enough to handle, but still warm. Good quality abalone emits a sweet fragrance like chestnuts when it's cooking. After making the body into sushi, we brush it with a sauce made by combining the abalone liver with egg yolk.

Surf Clam Scallop

Kobashira

These small scallops which have a great texture, a mouth-filling sweetness and the aroma unique to surf clams, are served in *gunkan* rolls, where the nori seaweed is wrapped around the sides of the sushi rice and the toppings are mounded on top. Surf clams have reduced drastically in number recently, and it's become difficult and expensive to get a hold of surf clam scallops too. We want the customer to enjoy the abundant flavor of this type of sushi, so even though they can be pricey we select surf clam scallops that are as big as possible.

Egg Cockle

Torigai

Egg cockle starts to become available in March, heralding the imminent arrival of spring. This shellfish has a tender yet firm texture and sweetness. Although its season is short, lasting only until May, the black, shiny, extended body is beautiful to look at. Many customers order it because they are fans of its appearance. We get it pre-shelled, and we always select the ones that have a large amount of innards.

Asian Hard Clam

Hamaguri

Plump simmered Asian hard clam has been a much beloved topping for Edomae (traditional Tokyo-style) sushi since the olden days. We get it in from the winter to the spring, before the clams start to spawn. Since we can get them on the market already shelled, we choose ones with big bodies. We especially like to get the ones from Ibaraki and Kagoshima prefectures. To give the clam a plump, juicy finish, we put it in a simmering liquid made of water, soy sauce and mirin, and gradually bring up the heat. We maintain the temperature at around 122 to 140°F (50 to 60°C) and simmer the clams slowly for about 30 minutes. When they are done, we leave them in the liquid for a whole day. We serve them brushed with a reduction of that simmering liquid.

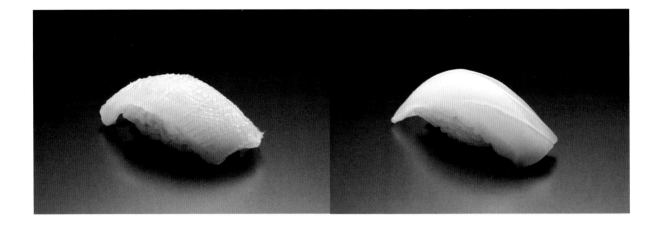

Bigfin Reef Squid

障泥烏賊

Aori-ika

With its rich texture, firm flesh, and strong sweetness and umami, bigfin reef squid is known as the king of squid and cuttlefish. As it is not caught much domestically, Japanese bigfin reef squid is very expensive.

Since this is a large squid with thick flesh, we age it in the refrigerator for about a week after breaking it down. It becomes sweet, tender and the umami becomes very pronounced. When it has become tender enough to meld well with the sushi rice, it has finished aging. In order to taste the distinctive sweetness of squid, we put a lot of cuts into the surface to increase the amount that is in contact with the tongue.

Golden Cuttlefish

墨烏賊

Sumi-ika

This cuttlefish is also called *koika* in Japanese. Translucent white golden cuttlefish are in season from the winter to early spring, but in late summer new cuttlefish (*shin-ika*), young golden cuttlefish, become available; their soft texture and elegant flavor are anticipated every year.

At Sushi Takahashi we mainly get them in from Kyushu, and try to choose ones that are as thick as possible. After breaking them down we rest them in the refrigerator for a whole day so that they become tender. When we slice them we usually make three cuts in the slices, but the number of cuts varies depending on the thickness and firmness of the flesh.

Octopus 蛸

Tako

Quality octopus has a lot of bounce, and its resilience can be judged by pressing on it. We get in octopus that weighs about 4½ pounds (2 kilograms), put it in a bowl while it's still alive and massage firmly with a large amount of salt for 30 to 40 minutes. When the sliminess on the body of the octopus has transformed into a watery liquid, it's done. After that it is steam-simmered slowly for about one hour.

Octopus becomes meaty and delicious in the winter, and the part next to the skin is especially tasty. There is a lot of gelatinous material between the skin and the flesh, which has a very rich flavor.

Sweet Shrimp

Amaebi

With their melting texture and strong sweetness, these shrimp are a popular sushi topping at our restaurant. We pull the heads off by hand, and peel them one by one, from the front, where the legs are attached, to the back, where the digestive tract is located. The tails are left on. Sweet shrimp goes off quickly, but since we want our customers to enjoy a strong sweetness, we do let them rest overnight in the refrigerator.

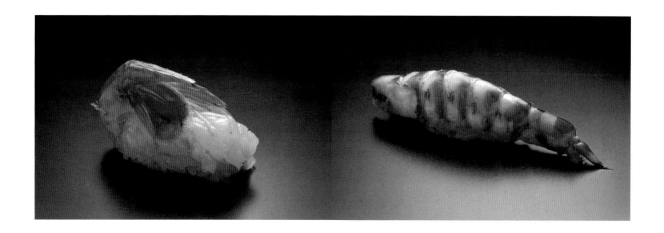

Botan Shrimp

牡丹海老

Botan ebi

These beautiful shrimp are reminiscent of
peony flowers (*botan*) hence the name. They
are available year round. If they are too fresh
they are too firm and springy, so we rest them
overnight in the refrigerator. We may even
freeze them lightly, depending on their
condition. Freezing helps the texture settle
down and the flesh become rich and thick.
We serve it with refreshing sudachi citrus
and salt. Sometimes we cure it with kombu
seaweed.

Tiger Shrimp

車海老

Kuruma ebi

The brown miso-like paste that is part of the
shrimp is left on when the shrimp is made
into sushi. Since the shrimp is eaten slightly
raw, it is only boiled for about 1 minute. This
takes place just before it is made into sushi,
and the shrimp is still warm. The rice is
slightly warm to match the temperature of
the shrimp, and although I usually use 12
grams of rice per sushi, for the shrimp I use
8 grams. I get the shrimp from a wholesaler
I trust, and it's an invaluable sushi topping
that is reliably available year round.

Mantis Shrimp 蝦蛄

Shako

This used to be caught in Tokyo Bay, and was known as a quintessential Tokyo-style sushi topping. It is cooked in a simmering liquid to imbue it with flavor, and served brushed with a reduction of that liquid. The best mantis shrimp are said to be the ones with eggs, available in May and June. Because simmered and marinated mantis shrimp have a lot of moisture and a rounded shape, they are hard to make into sushi, so they are pressed down with the palm of the hand to make them blend well with the sushi rice.

Salmon Roe

Ikura

At Sushi Takahashi we only serve this when we can get raw *sujiko* salmon roe in November and December. We break apart the membrane of the sac that holds the eggs and separate the eggs by hand. We then marinate the eggs in salted water that has a high concentration of salt, then shake gently in a sieve. This removes all pieces of the membrane, leaving only the eggs. After that we marinate the eggs in nikiri sauce (see page 126) for about 5 minutes. We keep to this timing so that the sauce does not penetrate the roe too much. We use up what we make on the same day.

Sea Urchin

Uni

The way sea urchin is prepared for sushi depends on its state when it is brought in. Its taste differs depending on the skill of the sea urchin seller—how much alum they use, how they finish it—so the most important thing is to establish a relationship with a seller you can trust. When it is turned into a *gunkan* roll (where the nori seaweed is wrapped around the sides of the sushi rice and the toppings mounded on top) the aroma of the crisply roasted nori seaweed and the rich flavor of the sea urchin go together very well. When we get in large-grained sea urchin, we sometimes serve it as nigirizushi rather than as a gunkan roll so that the texture can be experienced more directly.

Conger Eel

Anago

The season for conger eel is from early summer to fall, but I think the "rainy season conger eel" available in June is the fattiest and most delicious. A yellowish belly and a small head are the signs that the conger eel will have a good taste. After pre-processing it thoroughly (see page 105–6), it is simmered in a mixture of mirin, soy sauce and sugar for 25 to 30 minutes. It is broiled quickly just before it's made into sushi to bring out a nutty flavor, and then brushed with a reduction of the cooking liquid. During its peak season we sometimes serve it with salt instead of brushing on the reduction.

Hosomaki Thin Sushi Rolls

Sushi rolls, along with *tamagoyaki* omelet, are a favorite way to finish up a sushi meal. Nori-wrapped sushi rolls have a different appeal from nigirizushi. From cucumber rolls (*kappa maki*), tuna rolls (*tekka maki*), dried gourd strip rolls (*kanpyo maki*), conger eel rolls (*anago maki*), pickle rolls (*shinko maki*) to scallop mantle rolls (*himokyu maki*), we serve a variety of rolls depending on the sushi ingredients we have on hand.

In the Kanto region around Tokyo, sushi rolls are called *norimaki*, but in the Kansai region around Osaka and Kyoto, they are called *makizushi*. However, when you say *makizushi* the Kansai region, this word refers to *futomaki* fat sushi rolls (see page 196). In the Kanto region sushi rolls are divided into two types depending on their thickness—thick ones are *futomaki* and thin ones are *hosomaki*. It's not just the naming that differs by region. In the Kanto area the *nori* seaweed is toasted before it's used, but in the Kansai area it's not.

The procedure for making a sushi roll is simple in theory. You place the nori on the rolling mat (*makisu*), spread rice on top, put the fillings on the rice and roll it up. But in practice it it's rather difficult. The rice gets stuck to your hands; the nori may slip or rip when you try to spread the rice over it; it's hard to center the fillings properly; if you roll the rolls too tightly they will be too tough. It takes an experienced and dedicated sushi chef to make sushi rolls that look beautiful when sliced and that fall apart in the mouth just like nigirizushi.

A sushi roll is made with one whole nori sheet. The size of the nori sheet for sushi rolls is fixed; for fat futomaki, the sheet is 7½ x 8¼ inches (19 x 21 cm), and for thin hosomaki the sheet is cut in half and measures 3¾ x 8¼ inches (9.5 x 21 cm).

There is an old rule for how to cut hosomaki thin sushi rolls. Most rolls are cut into six pieces. Up to the Second World War, kanpyo maki dried gourd strip rolls were cut into three pieces, but because there is always one piece left over if divided between two people, it came to be cut into four pieces. However, some sushi chefs still stick to the "cut kanpyo maki into three pieces" rule.

A *makisu* sushi-rolling mat has a front and back side. The side on which the bamboo sticks are smooth is placed facing up, with the strings on the edge furthest from you. For a hosomaki sushi roll, use a 3¾ x 8¼ inch (9.5 cm x 21 cm) nori sheet. Put the rice in the center of the nori sheet right up to the near edge, and spread it out while pressing down lightly. Do not spread it right up to the far edge, but leave enough space so that that edge overlaps the near edge when the roll is formed. Place the filling in the center.

1 Lift up the edge of the rolling mat to hold the nori seaweed in place.

2 Start rolling toward the far edge of the nori sheet.

3 Pull the rolling mat over so that the edge of the mat goes over the far edge of the nori sheet. Pull the rolling mat toward you firmly while rolling the sushi. Press down to form the roll.

4 Take the rolling mat off and tidy up the ends of the sushi roll. Cut into individual pieces.

Futomaki Fat Sushi Rolls

Futomaki or fat sushi rolls tend to be eaten in the Osaka area of Japan rather than the Tokyo area. They are often made for takeout rather than eating in a restaurant. Originally they were made with a filling of freeze-dried tofu (*koya dofu*), shiitake mushrooms, dried gourd strips (*kanpyo*) and the parsley-like herb known as *mitsuba*, but these days extravagant futomaki made with *tamagoyaki* omelet and various types of seafood or fish are available too.

If nigirizushi is the type of sushi that typifies the Tokyo region, in the Osaka and Kyoto region sushi means *hakozushi* (sushi in a box), *oshizushi* (pressed sushi), or *futomaki*, fat sushi rolls. One theory for the prevalence of futomaki in the Osaka and Kyoto region is that there are a lot of temples and shrines in this area, and the futomaki is closely connected to Buddhist rituals: the futomaki of old were filled with Zen Buddhist vegan ingredients such as freeze-dried tofu (*koya dofu*), dried gourd strips (*kanpyo*), shiitake mushrooms and the parsley-like herb, *mitsuba*.

As time passed, freeze-dried tofu was replaced with *tamagoyaki* omelet, which is now common as a futomaki filling. More extravagant fillings such as shrimp, *oboro* (see page 148) and conger eel are used too. The fillings and form of futomaki—from round to square—differ depending on the chef.

A *makisu* sushi rolling mat has a front and back side. The side where the bamboo sticks are smooth is placed facing up, with the strings on the edge furthest from you. For a futomaki sushi roll, use a sheet of nori measuring 7½ x 8¼ inches (19 x 21 cm). Spread rice over the nori sheet right up to the near edge (the longer edge), pressing down lightly. Do not spread it right up to the far edge, but leave enough space so that the far edge overlaps the near edge when the roll is formed. Place fillings in the center in this order bottom to top: conger eel, shrimp, cucumber, tamagoyaki and kanpyo strips, as shown in the photograph.

1 Press down on the fillings in the center with your fingers while you lift up the edge of the rolling mat. There are a lot of fillings, so try to keep them in position.

2 Roll up the mat in one go so the near edge meets the far edge of the roll. Shift the rolling mat and press it hard to tighten up the roll.

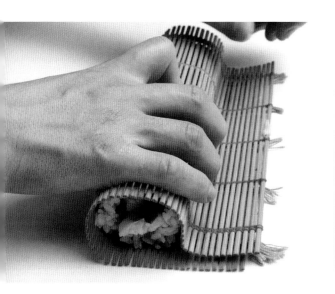

3 Press the rolling mat down to roll in the edge of the nori sheet. Round out the roll with your left hand as you give the roll one turn.

4 Take the rolling mat off and tidy up the ends. Cut into nine pieces, being careful not to squash the roll.

Classic Sushi Rolls

As long as we have the sushi filling ingredient on hand, we can turn anything the customer requests into a sushi roll for them. On these pages I will explain how we make some of the most popular sushi rolls at Sushi Takahashi.

Dried Gourd Strips

かんぴょう巻き

Kanpyo maki

The simple *kanpyo maki* roll defines Edomae (traditional Tokyo-style) sushi, and its flavor is totally determined by the way the dried gourd strips or are cooked in advance (see page 152). The strips are rinsed in several changes of water, then flavored quite strongly with sugar and soy sauce to match well with our sushi rice, which is on the sweet side. Kanpyo maki used to be served without wasabi, but recently serving with wasabi has become the rule. At Sushi Takahashi we ask the customer what they prefer before putting in any wasabi.

Cucumber

かっぱ巻き

Kappa maki

The simple, refreshing *kappa maki* is much loved as a perfect *shime*, the end to a sushi meal. The finely julienned cucumber has a nice texture, and some air is incorporated between the pieces when rolling, for a fluffy finish. Since we want the customer to enjoy a nutty flavor when they put the roll in their mouth, we add sesame seeds too.

Scallop Mantle and Cucumber

ひもきゅう巻き

Himokyu maki

The subtle bitterness and briny flavor of ark or red clam is enhanced by the refreshing fragrance of the cucumber. One can enjoy the crunchy texture of the scallop mantle and the crispiness of the cucumber.

Tuna

鉄火巻き

Tekka maki

Depending on which part of the tuna we have on hand that day, we adjust the amount we put in our tuna rolls. When it has a lot of fat we put in thin pieces, and when there is less fat we use thicker strips.

Tuna and Scallions

ねぎとろ巻き

Negitoro maki

For this roll we cut out the fatty tuna from the day's supply, and mince it together with green scallions. On some days it's an extravagant roll made with *otoro* premium marbled tuna belly. We mince the tuna rather roughly so that the customer can savor the texture. We use a type of scallion local to the Tokyo region, called *senju negi*, which has a nice fragrance and strong sweetness that really enhances the richness of the tuna.

Pickled Daikon Radish

お新香巻き

Oshinko maki

We use a type of pickled daikon radish called *bettarazuke* for our pickled daikon rolls, the same one we serve as an appetizer as part of our *omakase* chef's choice menu. In order to soften the strong taste of the bettarazuke, we soak it in water for a while, then in soy sauce and mirin. It becomes very well flavored, and well balanced with the sourness of the sushi rice.

Conger Eel and Cucumber

あなきゅう巻き

Anakyu maki

We use a crispy variety of cucumber called *hime kyuri* and finely julienne it for a good texture. We use this cucumber for other rolls too, not just because it's so firm and crispy but because it has a good fragrance. It goes very well with the rich nutty flavor of the conger eel.

Salted Plum and Shiso Leaf

梅しそ巻き

Umeshiso maki

A green shiso leaf is placed on the sushi rice, topped with a paste made by chopping up mildly flavored *umeboshi* salted plums from Wakayama Prefecture, then sprinkled with sesame seeds. The refreshing combination of the sour umeboshi and the green shiso makes this a popular sushi roll.

Fat Sushi Roll

太巻き

Futomaki

This *futomaki* is made by layering simmered conger eel, boiled shrimp, sweetly simmered shiitake mushrooms, cucumber, *tamagoyaki* omelet and cooked *kanpyo* gourd, in that order. This gives a soft melting texture, alongside the crispiness of the cucumber. We roll our futomaki so that the customer can enjoy the difference in these textures.

How to Cut a Hosomaki Thin Sushi Roll

Thin sushi rolls (*hosomaki*) are cut into four or six pieces as a rule. *Kanpyo maki* are cut into four pieces, while all others are cut into six pieces. In the olden days kanpyo maki used to be cut into three pieces, and some places still do this.

Cut into three pieces

- Dried gourd strip rolls (*kanpyo maki*) in the olden days

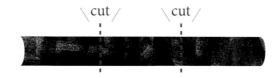

Cut into four pieces

- Dried gourd strip rolls (*kanpyo maki*)

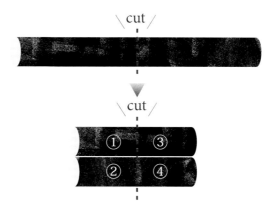

Cut into six pieces

- Tuna rolls (*tekka maki*)
- Cucumber rolls (*kappa maki*)
- Scallop mantle and cucumber rolls (*himokyu maki*)
- Tuna and scallion rolls (*negitoro maki*)
- Pickled daikon radish rolls (*shinko maki*)
- Conger eel and cucumber rolls (*anakyu maki*)
- Salted plum and shiso leaf rolls (*umeshiso maki*)

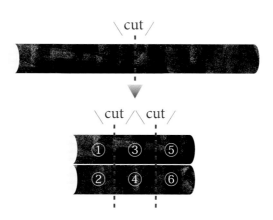

Nori Seaweed

When refined *nori* seaweed is used to make sushi rolls or *gunkan* rolls, it releases sweetness and a rich fragrance of the sea, melding with the umami of the sushi toppings and the sourness of the sushi rice in an indescribable way. Since nori used to be abundant in Tokyo Bay, it has long been an indispensable ingredient in Tokyo-style sushi.

Nori is made with seaweed such as Asakura nori (Pyropia tenera). It is mostly farmed, and its appearance and flavor differ depending on where it is grown. The season for nori is from November to February. The nori gathered during that period is called "first harvest" and has a uniquely rich fragrance and deep sweetness. The seaweed is processed into thin sheets like paper then dried to make nori.

The nori seaweed farms in the Ariake Sea, the Seto Inland Sea, Ise Bay and Tokyo Bay are well known. The farms in the Ariake Sea, off the coast of Kyushu, produce about half the domestic output of nori seaweed, and the nori produced here is characterized by its tender texture and strong umami.

Nori sheet sizes

Whole sheet
7½ x 8¼ inches
(19 x 21 cm)

Half sheet
7½ x 4 inches
(19 x 10 cm)

One third sheet
7½ x 2½ inches
(19 x 7 cm)

Nori has a shiny smooth side and a rough side. When making sushi roll, rice is placed on the shiny side, since it won't stick to it as easily.

Index

"Books to Span the East and West"

Tuttle Publishing was founded in 1832 in the small New England town of Rutland, Vermont [USA]. Our core values remain as strong today as they were then—to publish best-in-class books which bring people together one page at a time. In 1948, we established a publishing office in Japan—and Tuttle is now a leader in publishing English-language books about the arts, languages and cultures of Asia. The world has become a much smaller place today and Asia's economic and cultural influence has grown. Yet the need for meaningful dialogue and information about this diverse region has never been greater. Over the past seven decades, Tuttle has published thousands of books on subjects ranging from martial arts and paper crafts to language learning and literature—and our talented authors, illustrators, designers and photographers have won many prestigious awards. We welcome you to explore the wealth of information available on Asia at **www.tuttlepublishing.com**.

Published by Tuttle Publishing, an imprint of
Periplus Editions (HK) Ltd.

www.tuttlepublishing.com

SUSHI NO SCIENCE
Copyright ©2020 Jun Takahashi, Hidemi Sato, Mitose Tsuchida.
English translation rights arranged with Seibundo Shinkosha
Publishing Co., Ltd., through Japan UNI Agency, Inc., Tokyo

Japanese edition Editor: Mitose Tsuchida
Designer: Miho Takahashi
Photographer: Ryoichi Yamashita
Editing Cooperation: Chiyoko Iijima, Hiroko Shinbori
Special thanks to Kei Zenimoto, Miyuki Okada, Noi Maeshige

English translation by Makiko Itoh. English translation
copyright©2022 Periplus Editions (HK) Ltd.

ISBN: 978-4-8053-1713-6

25 24 23 22
10 9 8 7 6 5 4 3 2 1

Printed in China   2207EP

Distributed by

North America, Latin America & Europe
Tuttle Publishing
364 Innovation Drive
North Clarendon, VT 05759-9436 U.S.A.
Tel: 1 (802) 773-8930
Fax: 1 (802) 773-6993
info@tuttlepublishing.com
www.tuttlepublishing.com

Japan
Tuttle Publishing
Yaekari Building 3rd Floor
5-4-12 Osaki
Shinagawa-ku
Tokyo 141-0032
Tel: (81) 3 5437-0171
Fax: (81) 3 5437-0755
sales@tuttle.co.jp
www.tuttle.co.jp

Asia Pacific
Berkeley Books Pte. Ltd.
3 Kallang Sector #04-01
Singapore 349278
Tel: (65) 6741 2178
Fax: (65) 6741 2179
inquiries@periplus.com.sg
www.tuttlepublishing.com